Python Data Analytics

How to Learn Data Science and use Machine Learning. Introduction to Deep Learning to Master Python for Beginners

Tony f. Charles

Table of Contents

Introduction

Data is an essential part of the Information Technology ecosystem and is utilized to perform multiple operations in Machine Learning and Data Science. In order to analyze data for different types of predictions and business operations, it is mandatory to focus on mathematical models, graphs, data insights, databases, and statistics for developing deep learning models. Python programming language is considered as the best source for developing data science and deep learning models. Being a general-purpose programming language, Python is widely being used to gain insights from data and also serves as a powerful language to store, access and manipulate data in lists.

Python programming language is easy to understand, implement and interpret because it is an exceedingly powerful and effective general-purpose language. Over time, there have been several tools and integrated development environments created for data science and data analytics which support Python. Learning Python data science is also considered as the process of gaining knowledge and insights from diverse and huge datasets by analyzing, processing and organizing data. Programming of data science is flexible but involves the application of highly complex mathematical processes for which beginners are required to learn the basics of Python programming language.

Data science is based on complex algorithms and models for which a powerful programming language is required to handle mathematical processing.

Chapter 1: Python Data Science and Machine Learning

Artificial Intelligence, Machine Learning, and Data Science are the most commonly used technologies that are capable of performing complex operations and also bring long term benefits to businesses and industries. Over the past few years, researchers and developers have been working on creating machine learning models and algorithms that have the power to make accurate predictions and get trained by utilizing input data. Machine Learning is a data-driven system development algorithm that is based on data analysis, feedback, and data models which also help in refining algorithms for improving model accuracy and performance. Mainly, the machine learning systems analyze data to detect patterns and make accurate predictions by applying the predefined rules.

Data science is associated with data representation and scientific methodologies to transform algorithms for developing new solutions. By utilizing structured and raw data, data scientists make use of algorithms, mathematical models, and statistics to derive a specific solution. Generally, data science is based on the processes of data extraction, data cleansing, visualization, analysis and actionable insights generation. Furthermore, the approach also helps in predicting and understanding user behavior or recommendations. Machine learning is a major part of data science because it inherits aspects from algorithms and statistics to process the generated data and information extracted from multiple resources.

When it comes to dealing with enormous amounts of data, machine learning and data science algorithms are implemented together for processing information and gaining actionable data insights. It is mandatory to obtain knowledge about probability, statistics and technical skills to create data science models with complete functionality. Machine learning is also a part of artificial intelligence and is capable of performing major tasks such as data extraction, processing, and loading.

In order to develop state of the art and high performing data science models, developers are required to upgrade themselves with new skills and programming techniques. This includes in depth understanding and implementation of supervised and unsupervised techniques. In particular, data science covers major topics like data integration, distributed architecture, data visualization, and deployment in production model.

Why Learn Python for Data Analysis?

Python is an essential language for data analysis because it is flexible and easy to learn. Developers who want to create machine learning and deep learning models can use Python scripts and libraries which are easy to implement. Furthermore, the language is simple to learn which makes it ideal for beginners. Without spending much time and effort on coding, developers can utilize the functionality of Python to accomplish tasks without any hassle.

Due to its increased performance and functionality, Python has a large following and is vastly used in industrial and academic processes. There is a wide range of useful analytics libraries available for Python and users can approach to various community platforms to discuss their problems with other Python developers. Libraries such as Pandas, Numpy, and Matplotlib allow data analysts to carry out different functions smoothly.

Basics of Python for Data Analysis

Python is a general-purpose programming language that includes dedicated libraries for predictive modeling and data analysis. These built-in library packages can be used to import data from Excel spreadsheets and for processing sets for time series analysis as well. Pandas is a helpful Python Data Analysis Library that supports advanced manipulation through its powerful data frames and advanced numerical analysis features. Moreover, Pandas is built through NumPy which is one of the best libraries for data science development. Other major libraries such as SciPy, Scikit-Learn, and PyBrain are popular machine learning libraries that bring modules for developing data preprocessing and neural network models.

Better understanding and implementation of NumPy will make it convenient to work on tools like Pandas for which learning basics of Python programming language is necessary. Basics of NumPy include indexing of arrays, development with N-dimensional arrays, universal functions, statistical methods, and transposing an array to create data science models and algorithms.

NumPy

NumPy stands for "Numerical Python" and is a library that is comprised of a collection of multidimensional arrays. This library can be implemented to perform both logical and mathematical operations on arrays related to linear algebra and random number generation process. Data manipulation in Python is also performed through NumPy array and the latest Python programming tools such as Pandas are all based on this library. NumPy operations include access of data and subarrays to reshape, split and join the arrays.

In NumPy library, Ndarray is an N-dimensional array type that describes items of the same type which can also be accessed through a zero based index. Syntax to create ndarray using an array function in NumPy is defined as follows:

Numpy.array(object, dtype = None, copy = True, order = None, subok = False, ndmin =0)

For example:

Import numpy as np

A = np.array([4,5,6])

Print x

Output: [4,5,6]

2-D and 3-D arrays

2 dimensional and 3 dimensional arrays in NumPy can be defined by using the following basic syntax:

For 2 dimensional arrays:

C= np.array([3,4,5),(6,7,8)])

Print(c.shape)

(2,3)

For 3 dimensional arrays:

C= np.array([

      [[3,4,5], [6,7,8]],

[[7,5,4], [34,5,22]]

])

Print (d.shape)

(2,2,3)

Now, we can also create random arrays for which random function is used. Here is an example to specify the maximum value and size of an array in NumPy:

Random_array = np.random.randint(15, size =5)

Print(random_array)

Output: [1 3 56 98 45]

Boolean array

Array12_b = np.array([2,5,10], dtype='bool')

Arr2d_b

Array([True, False, True, dtype = bool)

Size and Shape

shape

print('Shape: ', arr2.shape)

dtype

print('Datatype: ', arr2.dtype)

size

 print('Size: ', arr2.size)

ndim

print('Num Dimensions: ', arr2.ndim) #>

Shape: (3, 4)

#> Datatype: float64

#> Size: 12

#> Num Dimensions: 2

Min, Max and Mean Operations on ndarray

mean, max and min

print("Mean value is: ", arr2.mean())

print("Max value is: ", arr2.max())

print("Min value is: ", arr2.min())

\#> Mean value is:

\#> Max value is:

\#> Min value is:

Adding Two Arrays

print(two_dim_array + two_dim_array)

Output:

[[4 2 6 15]

 [20 12 55 34]]

Function to convert an input to an array:

Numpy.asarray(data, dtype=None, order=None)[source]

Linspace and logspace functions:

Numpy.linespace(start, stop, num, endpoint)

Numoy.logspace(start, stop, num, endpoint)

SciPy

SciPy Python library is a built-in package which provides different resources to work on NumPy arrays. The library is mostly used in scientific computing, technical computing, mathematics and Engineering. It can operate on an array of NumPy library and also contains different types of sub packages which can be used to solve complex problems in scientific computation.

Packages:

Name	Description
Scipy.io	File input and output
Scipy.linalg	Linear Algebra
Scipy.special	Special Function
Scipy.interpolate	Interpolation
Scipy.stats	Statistics operations
Scipy.optimize	Optimization and fit.
Scipy.signal	Signal processing
Scipy.ndimage	Multidimensional image processing

Scipy.spatial	Spatial data structures and algorithms
Scipy.sparse	Sparse
Scipy.fftpack	Fast Fourier Transforms

Basic Functions

These are the basic functions that can be performed with SciPy library in Python:

Defining Data Types

import numpy as np

arr= np.arange(3, 5, dtype = np.float)

print arr

print " This is an Array data type :".arr.dtype

Output:[3. 4. 5.]

NumPy Vector

import numpy as np

list = [6,4,2,7]

```
arr = np.array(list)

print arr
```

Output: [6,4,2,7]

Installing the SciPy library:

```
Pip install scipy
```

Importing ScipPy library:

```
Import scipy
```

Single and Double Integrals

SciPy also supports general purpose integration which has only one variable present between two points. For example:

```
import scipy.integrate

f= lambda x: 12*x

i = scipy.integrate.quad(f, 0, 1)

print (i)
```

Output:

(6.0, 6.661338147750939e-14)

Source:

For double integral, dblquad function is used which is comprised of two variables with y being the first argument and x being the second argument.

```
import scipy.integrate

f = lambda x, y : 12*x

g = lambda x : 0

h = lambda y : 1

i = scipy.integrate.dblquad(f, 0, 0.5, g, h)

print(i)
```

Output:

(3.0, 6.661338147750939e-14)

Input and Output

To load and save a .mat file, we can use loadmat, savemat, and whosmat functions for a MATLAB file. For example:

```
import scipy.io as sio
```

14

```python
import numpy as np

vect = np.arange(10)

sio.savemat('array.mat', {'vect':vect})

mat_file_content = sio.loadmat('array.mat')

Print mat_file_content
```

Source:
https://docs.scipy.org/doc/scipy/reference/tutorial/io.html

Linear Algebra

Mathematics is the basic concept of Python. To perform calculations, SciPy offers fast linear algebra operations because it is created through BLAS and ATLAS LAPACK libraries. Method for solving a linear algebra system is defined as follows:

Problem: $1x + 2y = 5$

$\qquad 3x + 4y = 6$

Solution:

```python
# Import required modules/ libraries

import numpy as np

from scipy import linalg
```

```python
# Create input array

A= np.array([[1,2],[3,4]])


# Solution Array

B= np.array([[5],[6]])


# Solve the linear algebra

X= linalg.solve(A,B)


# Print results

print(X)


# Checking Results

print("\n Checking results, following vector should be all zeros")

print(A.dot(X)-B)
```

SciPy library also supports gradient optimization, integration, and special functions that are a part of numerical computation. Being an open source project, SciPy can also be used as a system prototyping and data processing environment like R-lab or MATLAB. Furthermore, high level classes and commands for data visualization and data manipulation increase the functionality and performance of SciPy Python library.

Pandas

Pandas Python library is designed with powerful data structures to support data analysis and data manipulation in data science. The library is mainly used for performing web analytics, statistics, finance and economics operations through Python programming. For processing and analysis of data, developers can consider Pandas library because it has the capability to load, organize, analyze, manipulate, and model the data for all kinds of datasets and inputs. Pandas is an efficient and fast DataFrame object which can work on both customized and default indexing.

Furthermore, developers can perform label-based slicing, sub setting, and indexing of large datasets through Pandas library. Other features include data alignment, integrated handling of missing data, reshaping of data sets and tools for loading data into memory objects. Generally, Pandas only supports Series and DataFrame data structures that are built through Numpy array.

Operations

Creating a data frame by using a dictionary of existing NumPy 2D arrays:

d_dic ={'first_col_name':c1,'second_col_names':c2 } df = pd.DataFrame(data = d_dic

Getting column names in a list:

Df.columns.tolist()

Reading data from a text file or CSV file:

df = pd.read_csv(file_path, sep=',', header = 0, index_col=False,names=None)

Reset an index to another list, array or an existing column:

new_df = df.reset_index(drop=True,inplace=False)

Remove a column:

Df.drop(columns = list of cols to drop)

Slice a dataframe for a given condition:

mask = df['age'] == age_value

or

mask = df['age'].isin(list_of_age_values)

result = df[mask]

Sorting values by column:

df.sort_values(by = list_of_cols,ascending=True)

Applying a function to all elements in a data frame:

New_df = df.applymap (f)

Generally, Pandas is based on two major components that are Series and DataFrame. Series is referred to as a column, whereas a DataFrame is a multidimensional table comprised of a collection of Series for Pandas.

Creating DataFrames

DataFrames in Pandas can be created in multiple ways. Here is a sample code for generating DataFrames through dictionary:

dict = {"country": ["Brazil", "Russia", "India", "China", "South Africa"],

"capital": ["Brasilia", "Moscow", "New Dehli", "Beijing", "Pretoria"],

"area": [8.516, 17.10, 3.286, 9.597, 1.221],

"population": [200.4, 143.5, 1252, 1357, 52.98] }

```
import pandas as pd

brics = pd.DataFrame(dict)

print(brics)
```

Source: https://www.learnpython.org/en/Pandas_Basics

Creating DataFrame through CSV:

```
# Import pandas as pd

import pandas as pd


# Import the cars.csv data: cars

cars = pd.read_csv('cars.csv')


# Print out cars

print(cars)
```

Indexing DataFrames

To index a Pandas DataFrame, we can use the simple technique of square bracket notation as follows:

```
import pandas as pd
```

```python
cars = pd.read_csv('cars.csv', index_col = 0)


# Print out country column as Pandas Series

print(cars['cars_per_cap'])


# Print out country column as Pandas DataFrame

print(cars[['cars_per_cap']])


# Print out DataFrame with country and drives_right columns

print(cars[['cars_per_cap', 'country']])
```

Importing Excel File

Importing an Excel file is possible through Python, for which we can use Pandas built-in library. We can use the read_excel function to import and manipulate data from a predefined Excel file. The syntax to import an Excel file in Python is defined as follows:

```python
import pandas as pd

df = pd.read_excel('path')

print (df)
```

Capturing Data

To import an Excel file into Python Pandas, we have to first capture the file path where the Excel file is located on your computer. For example:

C:\Users\Admin\Desktop\Sample.xlsx

Applying Python code:

```
import pandas as pd

df = pd.read_excel (r "C:\Users\Admin\Desktop\Sample.xlsx")

print (df)
```

Syntax to run the code:

```
pip install xlrd

import pandas as pd

df = pd.read_excel (r "C:\Users\Admin\Desktop\Sample.xlsx")

df = pd.DataFrame(data, columns= ['Price']

print (df)
```

Matplotlib

Matplotlib Python library is used to design and create 2D graphs and plots. The process is done with the help of Python scripts and it is based on a named pyplot. This pyplot provides extra features such as styles, font properties, and formatting. The package can be imported into Python script by using the statement as mentioned below:

from matplotlib import pyplot as plt

Developers can use Python Matplotlib library features to design plots, histograms, error charts, power spectra, scatter plots, and bar charts. The library provides complete functionality for all kinds of font properties, axes properties, and line styles as well.

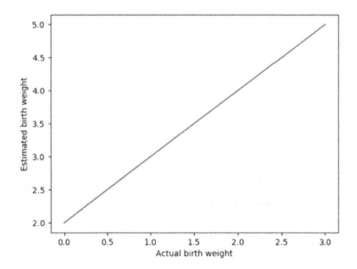

Source: https://data-flair.training/blogs/python-matplotlib-tutorial/

In the above graph, the methods xlabel() and ylabel() are used for setting labels for the x and y-axes. The values are taken from the list of parameters for y-axis whereas the values for x-axis are the four points 0.0, 1.0, 2.0 and 3.0.

Method to create pyplot interface:

Import matplotlib.pyplot as plt

Plt.plot ([2,3,4,5])

Data scientist can visualize the data to perform different types of data analysis operations. Here is an approach to plot a simple graph from matplotlib:

from matplotlib import pyplot as plt

plt.plot([1,2,3],[4,5,1])

plt.show()

Resulting graph:

Scatter Plot

For creating a scatter plot in Matplotlib, the following code based on the scatter method is used:

Fig, ax = plt.subplots()

ax. Scatter(iris['sepal_length'], iris['sepal_width'])

ax.set_title('Iris Dataset')

ax.set_xlabel('sepal_length')

ax.set_ylabel('sepal_width)

Line Chart

Line chart can be created by calling the plot method in Matplotlib as follows:

Columns = iris.columns.drop(['class'])

X_data = range(0, isis.shape[0])

Fig, ax = plt.subplots()

For column in columns:

      Ax.plot(x_data, isis[column])

ax.set_title('Iris Dataset')

ax.legend()

Chapter 2: Basics of Python

Python IDE's

An Integrated Development Environment is a tool which provides facilities like build automation, testing, code lining and debugging for different programming languages. Python IDEs are best suited for developing machine learning and deep analytics models. Here are some of the best IDEs for Python programming:

Sublime Text

Sublime Text is an amazing code editor that provides high customizability and is best for beginners. Along with other popular programming languages, Sublime Text also supports Python execution and comes with a predefined support for the language. The editor can be downloaded free of cost and is considered as a full-fledged Python development environment. Sublime Text packages are written in Python programming language which provide a wide range of extensions and packages to support complex programming.

Atom

Atom is an open source integrated development environment designed and developed by Github. Users can download and install the IDE along with predefined development packages such as linter-flake8 and python-debugger. Being highly customizable, users can install packages and set up the environment to meet their development requirements.

Eclipse

Eclipse is an all-rounder integrated development environment that is available for Windows, Linux, and OS X. The tool has a rich marketplace of add-ons and extensions which makes it suitable for machine learning and Python development. Furthermore, PyDev extension allows the developers to perform Python debugging and utilize code completion facility as well.

Getting Starting with Python

Basic Syntax

For writing your first Python program, you are required to be well aware of the basic syntax and requirements of Python programming language. A Python program can be written and executed in two basic modes which are known as Interactive mode and Script mode. In Interactive mode, developers are supposed to write a program and execute it, whereas in the Script mode, files and code can be saved and accessed through Python program (.py file).

Identifiers

Identifiers are used to identify a module, class, function, or a variable in a program. In Python programming language, an identifier can be a letter from A to Z or from a to z followed by zero or more digits, underscores, or letters. Furthermore, Python language does not allow characters such as %, $ or @ within identifiers. Being a case sensitive language, programmers need to carefully place identifiers to execute the program without any error.

Python syntax can be executed by writing the following line in the command line:

>> print("Hello world!")

Hello world

Variables and Data Types

Similar to other major programming languages such as Java, C and C++, Python has predefined data types and rules for using variables. For Python programming, you must remember that a variable can have both short and descriptive variables like x, y, age or year. A variable name should always start with a letter and cannot start with a number. Moreover, variable names are case sensitive in Python and developers need to be careful when declaring variables in the program.

Data Types

Python has built-in or default data types which include text, numeric, sequence, mapping, Set and Boolean and Binary type. To get the data type in Python programming language, "type()" function can be used in the program.

Here are some examples to set data types in Python:

Sample	Data Type
x = " Python"	Str
x = 5	Int
x = 5.0	float
x = range (5)	range

x = ("Red", "Blue")	Tuple
x = ["Red", "Blue"]	list
x = True/False	Boolean
x = b "Python"	bytes

Decision Making and Basic Operators

Decision making is an essential part of any programming language because it specifies the program to take actions according to the given conditions.

If statement

Syntax:

if expression:

      statement

Sample program:

```
#!/use/bin/python

Var1 = 50

if var1:
```

```
        print"1- Expression value"

        print var1

var2 = 0

if var2:

        print "2- Expression value"

        print var 2

print "Value:"
```

If-else statement

Syntax:

```
if expression:

        statement

else:

        statement
```

Nested If statements

In a nested if statement, we can have an if, elif and else present within another if, elif and else statement. The syntax for implementing this statement is defined as follows:

```
If expression1:
```

Statement(s)

if expression2:

statement(s)

elif expression3:

statement(s)

else:

statement(s)

Functions and Modules

Python has built-in functions which can be used to create complex machine learning and deep learning models. Built in functions are also known as user defined functions. For defining a function in Python programming language, we can use the syntax as described below:

Def function name(parameters) :

"function docstring"

function suite

return [expression]

For example:

Def printme (str):

"Sample string passed into a function"

print str

return

Modules in Python programming allow developers to organize their code and develop code modules that can be used further in the program. A module is also referred to as a file made up of Python code which includes arbitrarily named attributes, classes, variables and functions. For example:

def print func(parameter):

print "Sample: ", parameter

return

Furthermore, we can also import an existing module into the Python source code by using the import module support. Here are some of the import statement modules for Python programming language:

- import statement
- from.. import statement: from modname import*

Object Oriented Programming

Python is based on object-oriented programming modules which enables developers to perform different tasks through classes and objects. In OOP, a class is a user defined prototype which is defined for an object and contains a set of attributes, data members, class variables and instance variables. A class variable is shared with each instance of the class and is usually defined outside the class method. Furthermore, class variables cannot be used more often as compared to instance variables.

Instance variable is defined inside a method and only belongs to the current instance of a class. In object-oriented programming, function overloading approach is referred to as the implementation of more than one behavior to a specific function. To implement classes in a program, we are required to make use of objects and methods in the class definition. Here is the syntax to create a class in Python:

Class ClassName:

"class documentation string"

Class_suite

Sample student class in Python:

```
class Student:
  'Base class for all Students"
  empCount = 0
```

```python
def __init__(self, name, Grade):

    self.name = name

    self.grade = grade

    Student.stuCount += 1


def displayCount(self):

    print "Total Students%d" % Student.stuCount


def displayStudent(self):

    print "Name : ", self.name,  ", Marks: ", self.marks
```

To access class attributes, we can use the following syntax:

stu.1displayStudent()

stu.2displayStudent()

print "Student %d" % Student.stuCount

In a Python class, there are several built-in attributes that can be accessed by using the dot operator. For example, dict, doc, name, module and bases.

Class Inheritance

In object-oriented programming, a class can be created by deriving it from an existing class. The child class inherits the attributes from its parent class and they can also be used to override data members, functions, and methods from the parent class. Furthermore, the derived classes are the same in functionality as their parent class. For example:

class A: // Class A definition

..

class B: // Class B definition

..

class C(A, B): //Subclass A and B

Python syntax:

class SubClassName (ParentClass1[, ParentClass2, ..]):

    "class documentation string"

    Class_suite

Source:
https://www.tutorialspoint.com/python/pdf/python_classes_o
bjects.pdf

Regular Expressions

Regular expression or RegEx is referred to as the sequence of characters which is implemented to create a search pattern. For developing machine learning and data analytics models, regular expressions are widely used for pattern matching and training of models. Python comes with a built-in regular expression module which is also known as re module or RegEx module. To import the module, we can use the "import re" statement in the program.

The re module is comprised of different functions which can be used to search a string for match. For example, search, split, sub and findall are the major functions that are used for pattern matching and learning in machine learning models.

Implementation:

findall () function

import re

str = "Machine learning"

x = re.findall("in", str)

print(x)

Search() function

```
import re

str = "Machine learning"

x = re.search("\s", str)

print("Position of first white-space character:", x.start())
```

Split () function

```
import re

str = "Machine learning"

x = re.split("\s", str)

print(x)
```

Match and Search functions

Match function has the capability to match re pattern to the string. The syntax for match function is defined as follows:

```
re.match(pattern, string, flags=0)
```

In the search function, the first occurrence of re pattern is searched within optional flags and the string. The syntax for search function is defined as follows:

```
re.search(pattern, string, flags=0)
```

Furthermore, regular expression literals can also include an optional modifier. The optional modifier has the capability to control different aspects of matching and they are also considered as an optional flag.

Exception Handling

An exception occurs during program execution and can disrupt the smooth flow of program instructions. When an exception occurs in a Python program, it can be handled through 'try' and 'except' statements as explained below:

try:

    statements

except Exception 1:

    //if exception 1 occurred, execute this block

exception 2:

    //if exception 2 occurred, execute this block

else

No exception occurred

There are different exceptions and assertions which can occur in a Python program. For example: Exception, StopIteration,

SystemExit, StandardError, OverflowError, ArithmeticError, ZeroDivisionError, AssertionError, ImportError, KeyboardInterrupt, LookupError, IndexError, KeyError and NameError. It must be noted that a single try statement can have various except statements and they are only used when the try block has statements that might throw any type of exception. Furthermore, the Python program might also execute a generic except clause and handle any type of exception.

File Handling

File handling is an essential part of every web or desktop application. The approach is used to create, read, update and delete files from the database of the program. In Python programming, file handling is generally performed with open() function and includes filename and mode parameters.

Opening a File

To open a file through a Python program, we can use four different modes defined as follows:

Read: Opens file for reading and initiates an error in case the file does not exist.

Write: Opens file for writing and automatically creates a file if it is not available.

Append: Opens file for appending and creates if not available.

Create: Creates the required file and initiates an error if the file already exists.

Basic syntax for file handling operations:

To open a file: f = open("samplefile.txt"o

To open a file on server:

f = open("samplefile.txt", "r")

print(f.read())

Closing a File

f = open("Filename.txt","r")

print(f.readline())

f.close

Writing into Existing Files

f = open("samplefile.txt", "a")

f.write("New content")

f.close()

f = open("samplefile.txt", "r")

print(f.read())

Create new file: f = open("Newfile.txt", "x")

Deleting Files

To remove or delete a file in Python, you are required to import OS module for which os.remove() function is recommended. The syntax for deleting or removing a file in Python programming language is defined as follows:

import os

os.remove("Samplefile.txt")

Deleting a Folder

To delete a specific folder, we can use the following syntax:

import os

os.rmdir("Folder")

Chapter 3: Data Handling

Importing and handling datasets are the key functionalities of machine learning and artificial intelligence models. In Python programming language, there are different approaches and techniques that could be implemented to create data science projects and perform data handling operations. Comma Separated Value (CSV) files are the best suitable file format for storing and transferring data. Python provides the ability to read, write, and manipulate data to and from CSV files through Pandas library and data frames which makes it easier for data scientists to design and build machine learning models.

Importing Data with CSV files

Before building machine learning models, data scientists have to find the best suitable ways to gather and utilize datasets so that the models could be trained properly. Comma Separated Value (CSV) files are the ultimate source to import and export data for machine learning models. In Python programming language, Pandas library is used to deal with operations for importing and loading CSV files. Before using the file system, it is mandatory that you know where the data is located and what is the current working directory. All the information and data in computers is stored in directories which are generally known as folders.

There are different factors which need to be focused when importing data from CSV files. A CSV file has a predefined header that helps in assigning names to each column of data and in case the header is not available, you will have to define the names and attributes manually. Furthermore, you can also explicitly specify whether or not your CSV file had a header when loading the data. Generally, CSV files have a "#" sign at the start of a line which is used to indicate comments in the file. Depending upon the method, we can use different comments and characters to give information regarding the CSV file.

Loading CSV Files

CSV files are an essential part of machine learning models for which Python API comes with a predefined CSV module and reader() function to lead CSV files. After the loading is complete, the CSV data can be converted into a NumPy array to be used for building machine learning models.

Function to load CSV data through NumPy:

#load CSV

import numpy

filename = "Samplefile.csv"

rawdata = open(filename, 'rt')

```
data = numpy.loadtxt(rawdata, delimiter=",")
```

```
print(data.shape)
```

Function to Load CSV Data Through Pandas

We can also import data or CSV files through Pandas read.csv() function which is best suitable for building machine learning models. The syntax to implement read.csv() function is defined as follows:

```
#load CSV from Pandas
```

```
import pandas
```

```
filename = 'Samplefile.csv'
```

```
data = pandas.readcsv(filename, names= names)
```

```
print(data.shape)
```

Loading CSV File Data through Python Standard Library

Python language comes with a predefined API which provides reader() function and CSV module to load CSV files into the program. Once the data has been loaded, the CSV file can be converted into a NumPy array for utilizing it in machine learning models. Basic syntax for loading CSV file data through Python standard library is described as follows:

```
#load CSV

import csv

import numpy

filename = "Samplefile.csv"

rawdata = open(filename, 'rt')

reader = csv.reader(rawdata, delimiter=',')

x = list(reader)

data = numpy.array(x).astype('float')

print(data.shape)
```

Source: https://machinelearningmastery.com/load-machine-learning-data-python/

File System

Importing CSV files and data is possible by using Pandas and Python standard library. Before starting with importing data, it is mandatory that the developer is aware of file system location of data and the current working directory. 'ls' command is used to list all content in the current working directory whereas the 'cd' command gives you the name of the sub directory in which you can change your working directory. Furthermore, 'pwd' command can be considered to print the path of your current working directory and '..' command to navigate back to the parent directory of your current working directory.

To execute Shell commands directly from IPython, we can use IPython console which includes various magic command lines capable of performing multiple operations with a single command. When importing external files, we are required to focus on some important aspects to avoid any problems in execution of the program. You must make sure that data type variable is in a consistent date format and consider special values as missing values. Furthermore, check whether the header row is present or not and make sure that no truncation of rows occurs while fetching external data.

Importing Data File from URL

Here is the simple Python syntax to import file from URL in read_csv() function:

sampledata = pd.read_csv(http://sampleurl/file.csv)

Importing R data file

To import R data file, we can use pyreadr package and load .Rds and .RData format files from the R data frame by using the following syntax:

import pyreadr

```
result = pyreadr.read_r('C/desktop/sample.RData')

print(result.keys()

df1 = result["df1"]
```

Import Data from SQL Server and Tables Stored in SQL

We can read information and data from SQL Server by building a connection for which database details including server and user ID are required. Python syntax for importing data from tables in a database is defined as follows:

```
import pandas as pd

import pyodbc

conn – pyodbc.connect("Driver={SQL Server};Server=servername;UID=username;PWD=password;database=RCO_DW;")

df = pd.readsqlquerry('select*from dbTable WHERE AGE > 20', conn)

df.head()
```

Summarizing Data

Python gives us the power of packages, libraries, and data frames to perform manipulation and aggregation on data sets. Pandas library has built in functions which allow programmers to split a specific data set into subsets on a known criterion. Furthermore, you can also apply a function or a set of functions in your code to combine different results together. The goal of Pandas library is to perform data analysis by giving appropriate functions and data structures.

Splitting Data

After the data has been loaded, we can divide it into groups for which the following Python syntax is recommended:

bytreatment = data.groupby("Treatment")

bytreatment["Relalative Fitness"].describe()

Application of Data Functions

Grouped data can be manipulated into different forms by using statistical techniques in machine learning and deep learning models. In this regard, the describe() method is used to produce statistics for grouped data such as mean(), median() and max(). Furthermore, other arbitrary functions can also be applied over groups of data by using aggregate agg() method . For example:

bygroup.treatment["Sample"].aggregate(np.sum)

Or

```
bygroup.treatment["Sample"].aggregate(np.sum,      np.mean,
sp.std, len])
```

Furthermore, JSON files can also be used to store and manipulate data as text in human readable format. Pandas library comes with built in JSON files for which read_json function can be used. JSON is also known as JavaScript Object Notation and is saved with .json extension.

To input data using JSON file, we can use the following Python syntax:

```
import pandas as pd
```

```
data = pd.read_json('file/input path.json')
```

```
print (data)
```

Source: https://www.shanelynn.ie/summarising-aggregation-and-grouping-data-in-python-pandas/

Similarly, JSON function can also be used to read specific columns and rows from a CSV file. Pandas library supports read_json function which is implemented to read specific columns and rows after the JSON file is loaded into the DataFrame. Moreover, we can also use the .loc() method to load JSON file which is also known as the multi-axes indexing method.

Groupby method returns a groupby object which originally describes how the rows of original data have been split. The output of aggregation and groupby operations are different for Pandas Dataframes and Pandas Series for which we have to select the operation column separately. Moreover, the groupby output will be based on an index or multi-index rows depending upon the selected grouping variables.

Python Aggregation

Aggregation is generally performed through NumPy and Pandas libraries in Python. In most of the cases, the file data is not of a similar type or format and we are required to combine or group data into sets for further processing. However, in most of the cases, an aggregation function includes different rows combined together by the implementation of statistical algorithms like count, maximum, average, mean, mode, or median. In Python, data is aggregated to ensure the privacy of datasets and make it easier to analyze.

The most important aspect of using data aggregation is to meet legal and privacy concerns for a machine learning model. It is required that the data should be called to the group by using groupby() function to map values. The values can then be indexed and rely on the transform() function to develop aggregated data through NumPy and Pandas algorithms in

Python programming language. Sample program showing aggregation in Python:

```python
import pandas as pd

import numpy as np


df = pd.DataFrame(np.random.randn(10, 4),

        index = pd.date_range('5/4/2010', class=5),

        columns = ['1', '2', '3', '4'])


print df


r = df.rolling(window=3,min_class=2)

print r
```

Source: https://www.w3resource.com/python-exercises/pandas/python-pandas-data-frame-exercise-4.php

Unstructured Data

Data that is formatted in columns and rows can be simply converted into different structures to be implemented in the development of machine learning models. XLS, CSV and TXT files are the best examples of structured data because they have a predefined limiter and fixed width. On the other hand, there is data which does not have a specific format and is also known as unstructured data. Python libraries and predefined functions can be used to process unstructured files and utilize the data for processing.

The following example illustrates the reading of unstructured data in Python:

```
filename = 'input_data.txt'

with open(filename) as fn:

# Read each line

  ln = fn.readline()

# Keep count of lines

  lncnt = 1

  while ln:

    print("Line {}: {}".format(lncnt, ln.strip()))

    ln = fn.readline()

    lncnt += 1
```

Output:

Line 1: Python is a high-level programming language.

Line 2: It has a design philosophy that general-purpose interpreted,emphasizes code readability, notably using significant whitespace, interactive, object-oriented, and high-level programming language.

Line 3: It has grown from humble beginnings into one of the most popular programming languages on the planet.

Source: http://python-ds.com/python-processing-unstructured-data

Data Preparation for Analysis and Evaluation

Machine Learning and Artificial Intelligence models learn from the datasets and information they are fed with. Depending upon the labels and attributes of data, the models get trained to perform various operations and tasks in the future without human intervention. Data preparation is the first step that is performed after the data has been collected from one or more sources so that it is cleaned and transformed. Moreover, it is often merged with different sources having various levels of data and structures of data quality.

In order to create meaningful data insights, machine learning engineers and data scientists have to prepare data for analysis and outline the best sources to combine vital information and data.

How to Prepare Data

To prepare data for machine learning and predictive analysis models, we are required to focus on some simple approaches which will help us in collecting high quality data. After the objectives of model for predictive analysis have been defined, we can begin with data preparation. At first, you must identify your data sources because structured and unstructured data is available in different formats and types. Furthermore, data is mostly owned by a third party for which you need to acquire permissions to utilize the data.

Secondly, select the variables to add into your analysis for which you can start with multiple variables and eliminate the ones which offer no predictive values for the model. In most of the cases, derived variables have a greater direct impact on the model as compared to the raw variables which can in return affect performance of the machine learning model. To evaluate the quality of data, we need to understand the limitations and state of data because accuracy of the model is directly dependent upon data quality.

Although selecting and cleaning data is time consuming and requires a lot of hard effort, there are several effective data preparation techniques which can be followed to yield best results. Accuracy of machine learning models is directly dependent on the quality and accuracy of the training data.

How to Determine the Quality of Data

To explore the quality of input data, we need to understand the limitations and statistics that are required to operate the machine learning model with high accuracy. Make sure that the data is complete and perform any filtration before feeding the training data into the machine learning model. Furthermore, you are required to fill in the missing values or eliminate them if not needed. To perform analyzation and quality assurance, we can implement regression algorithms. Classification algorithms have the capability to analyze discrete data whereas the association algorithms can be considered for data having correlated attributes.

Datasets which are used to train and test the model should contain relevant business information. This will help companies to support their customers in a better way and provide them with the most suitable services as well. Smaller data files which have a good native structure can be opened through spreadsheets or editors, whereas larger or complicated datasets need to be handled with extraction or transformation software. Statistical adjustments can be applied to data which requires scale and weighting transformations. This will also help in cleaning data reviews for consistencies because generally inconsistencies may be found because of extreme, out of range or faulty logic.

In Big Data systems, preparing large datasets is time consuming and requires effort. To begin with the procedure, following data preparation rules on the sample data will reduce latency of iterative exploration and will make it easier to figure out large datasets. Data cleaning approach is used to find and eliminate errors in data.

Creating and Formatting New Variables

After the training data has been collected and finalized, the next step is to set up the variables which will directly respond to research queries and questions. Generally, datasets do not include measured variables and you are required to set up each variable individually. These operations include creating change scores, combining multiple categories of nominal variables, centering predictions and creating indices from scales.

Newly created and original variables need to be formatted properly for major reasons. Firstly, if you do not format a missing value or a dummy variable it will directly affect data analysis and predictions of your machine learning model. Secondly, it will save a lot of time and effort if a faulty variable is removed at first because setting all missing data codes and formatting date variables or numerical numbers will also remove any future discrepancies.

In Python development, we can take support from built-in libraries such as Pandas and NumPy to classify datasets and make separate groups. Data which is collected randomly features different categorical values and we need to label each variable before making it a part of training data. Based on the knowledge of business analytics goal and results of different data cleansing strategies, we can arrange the relevant data into a usable format without any hassle.

Underfitting and Overfitting

Underfitting and overfitting are two of the major issues which arise when building machine learning models and need to be overcome when handling input data. Underfitting occurs whenever a model is unable to detect relationships from data and it also indicates the essential variables to be included. On the other hand, overfitting begins whenever a machine learning model includes data having no predictive power and is only suitable for the given dataset.

Furthermore, if the machine learning algorithm or a statistical model captures vulnerable data it is known to be affected with overfitting. As a result, the algorithm shows high variance and low bias which in return affects its overall predictive powers. Overfitting and underfitting result in poor predictions on new data sets and greatly affect the performance of machine learning models. Nonetheless, we have to focus on validation and cross validation when building machine learning models to avoid overfitting and underfitting in each case.

Datasets which are used for the training of machine learning models are featured with multiple predictors. This helps businesses to avail accurate predictions and data insights in the long run from machine learning models.

Generalization

Machine learning models are known to learn from training data. The learning of target function from training data in the model is referred to as inductive learning because the aim of machine learning models is to apply specific rules and scenarios while generating outcomes. Generalization tells us how well the machine learning models have adapted the rules and information from training data and allows the model to make accurate predictions for the future. Overfitting and underfitting can surely make a machine learning model useless because they make it impossible for the models to learn from given datasets.

Generalization is also used to describe the ability of a model to react to new data and it usually happens when a model is being trained on a specific training dataset. If a model is trained well and accurately on training data, it will be unable to generalize the data and will make relevant predictions in future. Supervised machine learning models also make predictions based on the training data for which the outcome is already known.

Predictions and outcomes from the model are then compared with the actual data and the model's parameters are changed to achieve desired results.

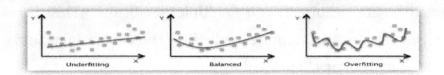

The above figure demonstrates underfitting, balanced, and overfitting graphs for a machine learning model. Based on the training data, the model notes that there is not a specific trend in data to capture relevant information, and because of this it is unable to make accurate predictions for new training data. This concept is known as underfitting and is illustrated by a straight blue line. In the middle, the line is representing a balanced model and shows the trend in data that could be easily generalized. Furthermore, on the right the line showcases a model which is too specific and inaccurately models the training data. This concept is also known as overfitting.

Chapter 4: Building Machine Learning Models

Interpreting machine learning and deep learning models is a complex task for which in depth understanding regarding data handling and ML algorithms is necessary. Nowadays, most of the businesses are relying on deep learning and AI models to drive their strategy and achieve best outcomes. Modern day examples of machine learning models are face recognition systems, self-driving vehicles and voice recognition systems such as Siri and Alexa. In-depth knowledge about statistics and linear recognition models is mandatory to design and build efficient machine learning models by using Python modules including Matplotlib, Pandas, and NumPy.

Data Science

Data science is a source of finding certain patterns in datasets and training data which are utilized by machine learning models to make accurate predictions. Initially, activities to build machine learning algorithms such as data mining were performed through basic statistical methods, but with the evolution of programming languages and modules, Python and

R deliver support to different computing packages that are based on statistics-focused approaches.

There are different steps involved in the collection of data. At first, data is collected from various sources and is then classified into structured and unstructured data categories. Next, the derived data is explored and transformed to remove any discrepancies. Aggregation and labeling of data are usually performed by a data scientist for which various machine learning and artificial intelligence algorithms are implemented. Once the goal is clear, we can set an evaluation protocol and decide how the ongoing progress will be measured. This will also help in determining the performance and capability of the machine learning model.

The process of training a machine learning model through data science techniques involves the selection of ML algorithms. There are different ways to deploy machine learning models for which we can make use of data modeling techniques.

Acquisition and Data Gathering

Before the training model is loaded with the annotated data, we must focus on predictive maintenance approaches. These approaches also help in upgrading performance of ML models and also improve their efficiency with time. With the availability of new data, we are given opportunities to make better decisions and consider best suitable variables for predictive maintenance.

Failure of machine learning models can also be minimized through root cause analysis. Predictive maintenance is generally performed through root cause analysis for which machine learning engineers have to determine the likelihood and occurrence of events. To get started with predictive maintenance, we need to feed high quality data into machine learning models and get the required insights as well. If there is a lot of usage information such as maintenance logs, it is compulsory that correct identifiers and variables are used to identify connectivity between the data sets.

DataRobot is a highly efficient automated machine learning platform that allows researchers and machine learning engineers to develop models that deliver accurate predictions and long-term insights. Furthermore, it also streamlines the data science process so that users get high quality predictions within a short period of time.

Data Pipelines

A machine learning system undergoes an extensive number of data processing workflows and has to perform multiple operations like cleaning and ingesting data. The process of developing and deploying continuously can lead to complications which need to be handled immediately to avoid any kind of unwanted scenarios. Machine learning pipelines have different parts and steps which are used to train the model. These models are cyclical and iterative because each step is directly linked with the other one. One after another, each process is repeated and to build better machine learning models, we need to derive scalable and accurate development techniques.

Data that is extracted from large datasets is also known as Big Data and is responsible for actionable insights in future. New connections and precise predictions can be performed with the support of data pipelines and it is not all about storing data, but we need to focus on achieving better outcomes. Today, most of the machine learning models are trained through neural networks and have the capability to perform a specific task in multiple ways. Machine learning deployment and development pipelines are separate from each other for which the data is supposed to be retrained or upgraded.

Furthermore, the pipeline approach also helps in releasing new versions and upgradations of machine learning models for which real time data is utilized. There are several tools, libraries and frameworks available for data scientists to work with pipeline methods. After the data has been collected and processed through data pipelines, the next step is to filter, aggregate and consolidate it before transferring the dataset to a permanent data store. Databases like SQL Azure and SQL Server are best suitable for handling machine learning data. Moreover, a machine learning pipeline helps to automate machine learning workflows and improves performance of models as well.

Challenges for Machine Learning Pipelines

Developing machine learning pipelines requires the data scientists to perform extensive research and evaluation. Generally, the process is divided into three sub categories which are data quality, data accessibility, and data reliability. Each of these categories is responsible for the performance, efficiency, and management of machine learning pipelines. Machine learning models need to be fed with accurate and complete training data so that they deliver the best suitable outcomes. The greater the availability of high-quality training data, the more accurate and reliable outcomes are achieved.

When it comes to data reliability, data scientists are supposed to determine the reliability of data and analyze its accessibility and source of generation as well. In most cases, implementation of a repository for data outcomes which serves as a single source of truth is necessary. Moreover, single source repositories allow machine learning models to run from multiple locations through a data center. Data reliability also helps in avoiding varying and duplicate versions of data so that analytical teams are always provided accurate and reliable data.

One of the major challenges that is being faced by data scientists for building machine learning model pipelines is data accessibility. Before the model is implemented into the system for commercial use, it undergoes deep cleaning and cleansing. This activity is performed to remove redundant and irrelevant data during the pre-analysis stage. In the development of machine learning model pipelines, feature extraction approach allows the developers to extract existing features along with their associated transformations into the latest formats to describe variances between data. Once the data is cleansed, it can easily be aggregated and combined with other cleansed data.

Object Storage in Machine Learning Pipelines

Machine learning pipelines tend to get better with time. True value occurs when more data points are collected along with different data assets which are collected from multiple sources. The activity of correlating new data formats into the data center is a complex task and various sets of applications are required to handle massive data load. In machine learning model development, cloud storage and object storage systems play a vital role because they serve a great purpose and support custom data formats as well.

Data analysts and scientists also consider mapping of statistical methods to solve key problems for object storage in machine learning models. For quick business implementation, data scientists prefer to store everything locally and not in a public cloud because it takes more time and effort to extract information when needed. There is an abundance of machine learning content and immediate access is mandatory to maintain the performance and efficiency of machine learning models. Furthermore, each step in the process is iterative and cyclical which makes it convenient to upgrade and manage the algorithms.

Architecture of Machine Learning Pipelines

Machine learning pipelines are designed and architected through a predefined model. As it involves batch processing and handling of data to perform different operations, a machine learning pipeline has special features which allow it to make accurate predictions and insights. A pipeline is comprised of different stages and each stage is fed with processed data from its preceding stage. In the preprocessing stage, scientists use data mining techniques for data preprocessing which also involves transferring raw data into an understandable format. Data taken from external resources in often inconsistent and incomplete for which various treatment procedures are applied to remove the inaccuracies.

Constructing pipelines gives several advantages and makes it easier to implement machine learning models. The units of computation for ML pipelines are quite easy to replace and are highly flexible as well. Upgrading or changing a single part of the system can be done without dismantling the entire system. Every part of computation can be controlled through a common interface and if any part is not performing up to the mark, engineers can scale that component independently as well. Furthermore, the functionality and performance of machine learning pipelines can be increased by adding extensions into the system.

Pipelines are based on the approach of overnight batch processing which includes collection of data, sending of data, and processing it through multiple channels to feed the machine learning models. Predictions and features in pipelines are highly time sensitive because its performance is directly dependent on online model analytics and offline data recovery. Online model analytics represents the operational component of the system and is generally applied for real-time decision-making approaches. On the other hand, the offline data recovery method represents the learning component of ML pipelines and utilizes the historical data to create machine learning models through batch processing.

Online and Offline Layers

Gathering and funneling the incoming data into storage is the first step of creating any kind of machine learning workflow. Without undertaking any transformation, we can have an immutable record of original dataset for which the data can be fed from multiple sources or obtained from other services as well. Generally, data scientists use NoSQL document databases to store large volumes of constantly changing structured and unstructured data.

Online ingestion service is the gateway to streaming architecture in machine learning pipelines because it decouples and completely manages the workflow as well. The information from data sources is processed and transferred to storage components for which the system ensures better reliability, low latency, and high throughput. Offline layers in the machine learning pipelines utilize ingestion services to confirm data flows into the raw data store. To perform this activity, a repository pattern is used to interact with a data service and also with the data store. As soon as the data is received and saved in the data store, it is automatically assigned a batch ID which allows efficient querying and traceability.

Ingestion distribution in machine learning pipelines ensures that there is a separate pipeline for each dataset and all of them are processed and managed independently. Furthermore, the data is partitioned within each pipeline to take benefit of multiple server cores and processors in the system. Furthermore, spreading the data preparation through multiple pipelines horizontally and vertically also reduces the overall time to complete the workflow.

For example:

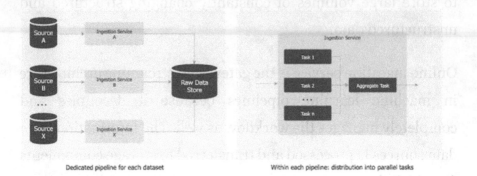

Dedicated pipeline for each dataset   Within each pipeline: distribution into parallel tasks

Source: https://towardsdatascience.com/architecting-a-machine-learning-pipeline-a847f094d1c7

As briefed in the diagram above, we can notice that ingestion services operate regularly on a predefined schedule or depend on a trigger. As it is supposed to fetch data from thousands of sources each day, the producer system automatically releases a message to the broker so that the embedded notification service gives prompt response to the subscription.

In both of these layers, we can see that a distributed pipeline is developed which examines the condition of data and searches for various trends, formats, differences and skewed data. Furthermore, it is mandatory that the correct design pattern is chosen before developing machine learning pipelines in order to ensure consistency and better outputs from training data.

Data Segregation

Data segregation splits the subsets of the given data in order to train machine learning models. Apart from training, data segregation also analyzes model performance and efficiency for the system. The machine learning systems are designed to utilize quality data and perform pattern prediction for data on which it is not trained. This allows ML models to deliver accurate insights and predictions on each scenario. There are several strategies to perform data segregation in machine learning pipelines. Data segregation is not separately a machine learning pipeline and is known as an API to facilitate specific tasks.

Model training of machine learning pipelines is usually performed offline because the schedule is strictly dependent upon the criticality of application. Moreover, service and maintenance time can also affect learning of a machine learning pipeline for which schedulers can be implemented.

Parallelization

Machine learning models have a dedicated pipeline which allows all of the models to run concurrently. To apply the parallelization technique, we are required to parallelize all of the training data which is partitioned. Each of the partitions has a copy of the original model and it is preferred that all of the fields of instance perform computation on their own. Furthermore, a machine learning model can also be parallelized by itself for which the model is completely partitioned. Each partition is responsible for handling and updating each portion of parameters. This approach is best suitable for Linear machine learning models such as SVM and LR.

Training of machine learning pipelines is implemented with slight error tolerance. The model training service is supposed to get training configuration parameters and hyper-parameters from configuration services. This approach allows the model to utilize the configuration service and fetch the training dataset from Data Segregation API. As a result, the dataset which is sent to all of the other models is complete and is based on the original configuration.

In machine learning model pipelines, the Model Evaluation Service is applied to request evaluation dataset from Data Segregation API. This activity is done for each model which is directly sourced from the model candidate repository and also applies relevant evaluators as well. As a result, the evaluation is saved back to the repository and becomes a part of the hyperparameter and iterative process techniques.

Importance of Metadata

Python programming language is best suited for the development of machine learning models and pipelines. Data scientists and analysts who are determined to achieve the best predictions and efficiency from ML models get support from Python libraries and functions. One of the major tasks for developing machine learning models is the extraction of metadata. Once a pipeline or model is trained sufficiently, it can be made operational for industries, businesses, and brands to yield accurate data insights.

Traditionally, file-based network attached storage (NAS) architecture was used to figure out data which had to be traversed with each operation. With thousands of directories waiting to be processed, the activity took a lot of time and effort. As a solution, object storage and ML training approaches were implemented in the architecture of artificial intelligence and deep learning models. In an object storage platform, data including text documents, files, or videos can be stored as a single object. To make things manageable, metadata is attached with the files which provides descriptive information regarding the captured data.

Model Evaluation

Evaluating a machine learning model is a crucial step of the development procedure. Although ML models yield satisfying results when trained on proper data sets, we are required to evaluate the performance, efficiency, and reliability to achieve best results in future. There are several evaluation metrics defined to examine the accuracy and response of machine learning models. We can see how the model generalizes and forecasts on unseen data as it directly affects the performance of machine learning pipelines as well. To evaluate the aspects in a better way, we need to understand how the model actually works and whether we can trust its predictions or not.

Generally, the methods for evaluating the performance of machine learning models are separated into two categories, namely cross validation and holdout. Both of these methods utilize a test data to evaluate model performance and it is never feasible to use the data which we used to build the model to examine it in future.

The following techniques are the best source of measuring performance and evaluating the efficiency of machine learning models:

Confusion Matrix

Confusion matrix is an approach which provides a complete detail of correct and incorrect classifications. For a confusion matrix, we need to remember a few key points so that the efficiency can be calculated properly. Accuracy is the part of the total number of correct predictions made by the model, whereas the positive predictive value is considered as the part of positive cases identified correctly. Negative prediction value in machine learning models is the part of negative cases which were identified correctly, whereas specificity identifies the proportion of actual negative cases that are identified correctly.

At first, we can take an N x N matrix and consider N as the number of classes for prediction as follows:

	Class1 Predicted	Class 2 Predicted
Class 1 actual	TP	FN
Class 2 actual	FP	TN

A confusion matrix can be examined through the following important terms:

1. True Positives - Occurs for cases in which Yes was predicted whereas the actual output is also the same.

2. True Negatives - Occurs for the cases in which NO was predicted whereas the actual output is also the same.

3. False Positives - Occurs for the cases in which Yes was predicted whereas the real output is NO.

4. False Negatives - Occurs for the cases in which No was predicted whereas the real output is YES.

Classification rate or accuracy for a machine learning model can be calculated from the equation below:

$$\text{Accuracy} = \frac{TP + TN}{TP + TN + FP + FN}$$

Taking the example of a cancer detection model, we can consider that the actual chances of having cancer are quite low for which a probability of 10 out of 100 is possible. We will never want to miss any patient in this case who has cancer but remains undetected. In this case, detecting every patient as not having cancer yields an accuracy of 90% for which the machine learning model can be held accountable.

F1 Score

The F1 score in machine learning and data analytics models is known as the harmonic mean of recall and precision. The score utilizes the contribution of precision and recall calculations to analyze the performance of a machine learning model. Moreover, if the model performs well in F1 score, it will have a higher ratio of making accurate predictions as compared to the model which has a lower F1 score.

Formula to calculate F1 score:

$$F_1 = \left(\frac{\text{recall}^{-1} + \text{precision}^{-1}}{2} \right)^{-1} = 2 \cdot \frac{\text{precision} \cdot \text{recall}}{\text{precision} + \text{recall}}$$

Logarithmic Loss

Logarithmic loss approach is used to evaluate the performance of a classification model. To evaluate logarithmic loss through mathematical calculation, we need take prediction input probability ranging from 0 to 1. With the increase of logarithmic log or log loss, the predicted probability changes from the actual label to minimize the end value.

PR Curve

Precision and Recall curve are the best way to represent properties of a classifier. PR curve is the curved formed between recall and precision for different threshold values. For example:

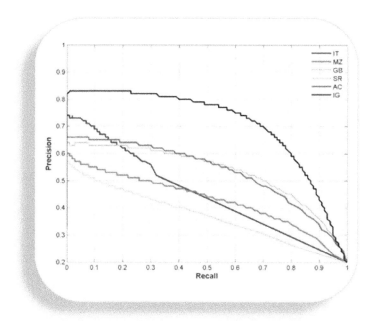

Source: https://github.com/MenuPolis/MLT/wiki/PR-Curve

From the above graph, we can notice that precision is represented by the fraction of blue circle or retrieved documents that are used as TP. Upon a low precision value, the system will have to search through different irrelevant searches to find the required value. Furthermore, we can repeat the search by eliminating an unwanted meaning of the searched word. For machine learning models, precision is considered as a measure of usefulness whereas recall is known as a measure of completeness.

Chapter 5: Machine Learning Algorithms

Before starting a data science or machine learning project in Python programming language, understanding the ideas, concepts, and functionality of ML models is compulsory. Whether you want to load data into the model or evaluate its performance, the parameters set in machine learning algorithms can help in achieving the best outcomes. As discussed earlier, data can be extracted, uploaded, and managed through Python libraries like NumPy and Pandas. In machine learning, the most commonly used format for data is known as Comma-Separated Values or CSV format, which is also applicable for storing and handling files.

Introduction to Model Handling

With the increasing demand in big data analytics and deep learning, machine learning has become a popular approach for solving real life and business problems. The approach is widely used in system development for various fields including health care, computational finance, computer vision, image processing, and computational biology. Furthermore, data science plays a vital role in automotive, energy production, and natural language processing systems.

The models are programmed to find natural patterns in data and generate insight for making accurate predictions in the future. Basically, machine learning models are divided into two major categories called supervised learning and unsupervised learning. Because machine learning models have the capability to find non linear dependencies between input data, we need to check before making any changes in our data because it can create cascading effects on downstream systems and model accuracy.

Linear Regression in Python

Artificial Intelligence and machine learning systems have the capability to handle large amounts of data which makes them best suited for powerful computers. Linear regression is one of the major parts of machine learning and deep learning algorithms because it is based upon the fundamentals of statistics and mathematics.

Regression

The term "Regression" refers to the search for relationships amongst variables in datasets. It is considered as a statistical measurement to determine the strength of a relationship between an independent variable, and the approach is widely implemented in the finance industry. Regression analysis is one popular technique used by researchers and data scientists to understand the phenomenon of interest and findings of different observations.

To implement regression in machine learning models, we are required to find a function that maps variables and features to others in an effective way. Dependent features are also known as dependent responses, outputs, or variables, whereas the independent features can be referred to as independent predictors, inputs, or variables in machine learning. Generally, regression problems result due to unbounded and continuous dependent variables for which the data needs to be handled with different techniques.

Why is Regression Important?

Regression is a useful approach to forecast a response by the support of new predictors and datasets. For machine learning models and deep learning analytics, linear regression is a widely used regression technique because it delivers great ease of comparing and interpreting results. Furthermore, implementation of linear regression in machine learning models is now possible with Python libraries and functions.

The below graph represents linear regression in machine learning models:

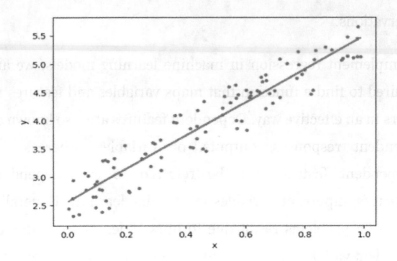

Equation to represent linear regression model:

$$Y = \theta_0 + \theta_1 x_1 + \theta_2 x_2 + \dots + \theta_n x_n$$

Python implementation for creating random dataset to train machine learning models:

import numpy as np

import matplotlib.pyplot as plt

generate random data-set

np.random.seed(0)

x = np.random.rand(100, 1)

y = 2 + 3 * x + np.random.rand(100, 1)

plot

plt.scatter(x,y,s=10)

plt.xlabel('x')

plt.ylabel('y')

plt.show()

Source: https://towardsdatascience.com/linear-regression-using-python-b136c91bf0a2

In linear regression model graphs, we can notice the error line between the observed and predicted values which is also known as regression line or the line of best fit.

Types of Linear Regression Models

Linear relationship

It is the linear relationship between feature variables and response in a machine learning model. Linear relationship can be described by the following graphs:

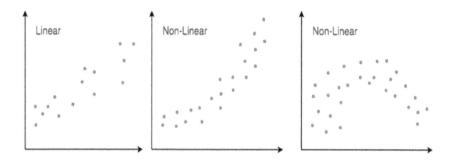

Homoscedasticity

Homoscedasticity is known as an error term that occurs as a result of a random disturbance between the dependent and independent variables.

Multiple Linear Regression

Multiple linear regression occurs in an event of linear regression between two or more independent variables in a machine learning model. The estimated regression function for two independent variables can be represented through the equation $f(x_1, x_2) = b_0 + b_1 x_1 + b_2 x_2$. If there are more than two independent variables, we can determine the value of estimated regression function through the equation $f(x_1, \ldots, x_r) = b_0 + b_1 x_1 + \cdots + b_r x_r$.

Polynomial Regression

Polynomial Regression is an essential part of linear regression because the polynomial dependence for inputs and outputs is considered as the polynomial estimated regression function. The equation to calculate polynomial regression is $f(x) = b_0 + b_1 x + b_2 x^2$.

Implementation

On a given dataset, we can use different Python libraries to implement linear regression. Here is the program to import all of the required libraries and read the dataset in Python:

```
import numpy as np

import pandas as pd

import seaborn as sns

import matplotlib.pyplot as plt

from sklearn import preprocessing, svm

from sklearn.model_selection import train_test_split

from sklearn.linear_model import LinearRegression

df = pd.read_csv('sample.csv')

df_binary = df[['Python',]]

df_binary.columns = ['Age', 'Year']

df_binayr.head()
```

Syntax for data cleaning:

```
Df_binary.fillna(method = 'fill', inplace = True)
```

Scikit Learn

Scikit-Learn is a built-in Python library which is exclusively designed for the development of machine learning models. The library provides complete support and execution for major machine learning algorithms including random forest, k-neighbors, and linear regression. Furthermore, libraries such as NumPy and SciPy can also become a part of Scikit-Learn Python library to develop state of the art and high performance machine learning models. Scikit-learning library is designed to make machine learning development easier through Python programming language because of its various data handling and plotting techniques that help to visualize data.

Loading Data Sets

Loading datasets is the first step of developing ML models through Sci-kit learn Python programming technique. Each process and activity in data science starts with loading data, and this approach is more suitable for observed data. Before loading data into the program, make sure it is free of any independencies or mistakes so that accurate data visuals and results could be attained. Furthermore, finding datasets is challenging, for which you can also create your own sets of data to implement within the Sci-kit learn algorithm.

To load data into the program, we are required to import datasets module from sklearn and implement the load_digits() method. Python syntax to load data:

#import datasets from sk-learn

from sklearn import

digits = datasets.load_digits()

print

The dataset's module includes other methods to load and fetch reference datasets and we can also consider this in the case of artificial data generators. Moreover, the dataset can be inherited through the UCI Repository as well.

Exploring Data

After you are done with loading data, the next step is to start exploring the dataset for which Python libraries provide simple methods to be implemented. Scikit-learn library does not provide information related to data and if you are importing data from another source, there is a slight detail given about data which can be used to generate insights during model development.

If you are using the read_csv() module to import data, you can have a dataframe which contains just the data. No information related to the dataset is given in this case, but you will implement head() and tails() methods to inspect data. Data exploration is an essential step in the development of machine learning or data science projects. Even a quick evaluation for data can give true insights related to quality and reliability of the datasets.

Predicting and Learning

Datasets including numbers, images, or text files can be examined through sklearn.svm.SVC estimator class. The estimator class in Python can be set by using the following syntax:

from sklearn import svm

clf = svm.SVC(gamma= 0.005, C =50)

In Scikit-learn library, the estimator for classification can also be implemented through fit(x,y) and predict(T) methods. For classifier, we can use the clf estimator which must learn from the model. Furthermore, the method is completed by passing the training set to the fit method in the Scikit-learn library and for the training set, we can use all images or text from our dataset.

How to Split Data into Training and Test Sets Through Scikit-learn

To assess a machine learning model's performance, we can divide the data set into two parts which can also be named as a test set and a training set. Training set is used to train the system whereas the test set is implemented to evaluate the trained or learned system. In Scikit-learn, we can apply train_test_split() method along with the random_state argument to split data sets in the program. For example:

from sklearn.cross_validation import

X_train, X_test, y_train, y_test, images_train,

images_test = train_test_split(data, digits.target, digits.images, test_size=0.25, random_state=42)

Creating a DataFrame

Before splitting, we are required to create a DataFrame for which importing Pandas library is mandatory. Python syntax for creating a DataFrame is defined as follows:

import numpy as np

from sklearn.preprocessing import MinMaxScaler

sampleData – np.random.randint(50, 100)

sampleData

scalar_model = MinMaxScalar()

feature_data = scalar_model.fit_transform(sampleData)

feature_data

Output for the above program:

```
In [22]: scalar_model = MinMaxScaler()
         feature_data = scalar_model.fit_transform(demoData)
         feature_data

         /anaconda3/lib/python3.6/site-packages/sklearn/utils/validation.py:475: DataConversionWarning: Data with input dtype
         int64 was converted to float64 by MinMaxScaler.
           warnings.warn(msg, DataConversionWarning)

Out[22]: array([[0.         , 0.27602906, 0.13174946, 0.17372881],
               [0.95081967, 0.75302663, 0.42548596, 0.05508475],
               [0.8989071 , 0.31234867, 0.32612391, 0.77118644],
               [0.38251366, 0.49394673, 0.        , 0.31144068],
               [0.7704918 , 0.22760291, 0.83585313, 0.875     ],
               [0.43169399, 0.52542373, 0.26133909, 1.        ],
               [0.20491803, 0.07021792, 0.31317495, 0.74798136],
               [0.83060109, 0.57869249, 0.16848652, 0.52118644],
               [0.98907104, 0.3220339 , 0.20986393, 0.15466102],
               [0.13934626, 0.        , 0.3650108 , 0.        ],
               [0.38251366, 0.58595642, 0.35205184, 0.56567797],
               [1.        , 1.        , 0.23324134, 0.20762972],
               [0.24590164, 0.62227603, 0.09071274, 0.53813559],
               [0.86338798, 0.7748184 , 0.15982721, 0.72669492],
               [0.1147541 , 0.63196126, 0.47732181, 0.87711864],
               [0.85519126, 0.95883777, 0.80345572, 0.59322034],
               [0.54644809, 0.93220339, 0.82289417, 0.70127119],
               [0.05464481, 0.1622276 , 0.91144708, 0.81355932],
               [0.60928962, 0.08232466, 1.        , 0.53601695],
               [0.46994536, 0.07263923, 0.75593952, 0.68008475]])
```

Splitting data into train and test:

from sklearn.model_selection import train_test_split

X_train, X_test, y_train, y_test = train_test_split(X,y, test_size = 0.50, random_state = 50)

Source: https://www.dataquest.io/blog/sci-kit-learn-tutorial/

Splitting and scaling are the most crucial steps in machine learning model development for which scikit-learn approach gives the best suitable methods to handle data sets.

Building Pipeline

Pipelines are the best source for feeding data to machine learning models. Raw data is entered into the pipeline to perform various operations for which we are required to standardize categorical data and continuous variables. The Python syntax to implement pipeline in a machine learning model is defined as follows:

```python
from     sklearn.preprocessing     import     StandardScaler,
OneHotEncoder, LabelEncoder

from     sklearn.compose     import     ColumnTransformer,
make_column_transformer

from sklearn.pipeline import make_pipeline

from sklearn.linear_model import LogisticRegression
```

Scikit-learn also provides different functions to run cross validation and parameter tuning. In cross validation, the training set is run multiple times to evaluate the performance and efficiency of models, whereas the grid search approach includes various hyperparameters to check the machine learning model. Logistic classifier is one of the best sources to tune an ML model and can also be used to speed up training.

Effective Data Visualization

Data visualization is one of the major aspects of machine learning and data science. To begin with construction of ML models through Python programming language, we need to understand each of the underlying dataset and explore variables in great depth. Effective data visualization is the core tool for designing and developing machine learning models with high performance and great efficiency. Python data visualization is done through Seaborn, Pandas, and Numpy libraries.

Three important considerations for data visualization are accuracy, clarity, and efficiency. Efficiency makes use of efficient visualization approaches to highlight specific data points, whereas accuracy makes sure that only appropriate graphical representation is taken to deliver the message. Furthermore, clarity portion makes sure that the given dataset is relevant and complete. This allows data scientists to study new patterns which are derived from data in specific places from the graph.

To install Seaborn, we can use the following syntax:

pip install seaborn

Types of Data Visualizations

Scatter Plot

Python programming can be used to design and create graphs of different categories. Scatter plots are the same as line graphs and we can utilize both vertical and horizontal axes to visualize the data points. As they are comprised of a large body of data, a straight line is formed because of the closer data points. Note that a stronger correlation between two variables yields a completely straight-line graph.

Details of Line Properties

Property	Value Type
Animated	True/False
Alpha	Float
Clip box	A matplotlib.transform.Bbox instance
Clip path	Patch
Linewidth	Float value in points

Implementation for Scatter Plot in Python:

import matplotlib.pyplot as plt

import pandas as pd

import seaborn as sns

import warnings

```
warnings.filterwarnings('ignore')
```

```
fig = plt.figure(figsize=(5, 10))
```

```
df = pd.read_csv('SampleData')
```

```
ax = sns.regplot(x="wt", y="mpg", data=df)
```

Histogram Plot

Histograms are the graphical representations for a probability distribution and can be created through matplotlib and bar chart function in Python. For example:

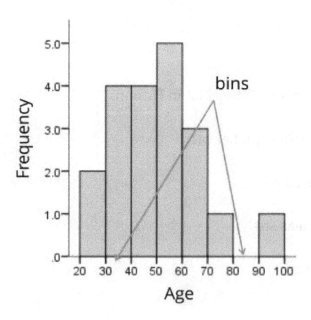

Python implementation:

```
import pandas as pd

import seaborn as sns


df = pd.read_csv('SampleData')


fig = plt.figure(figsize=(5, 100))

sns.distplot(df.Temp, kde=False)
```

Bar Plots

In Python, we can also create bar graphs or bar plots to display and compare the frequency or number of data. Remember that the data can be of different discrete categories because bar plots have more frequency as compared to other types of graphs. Bar plots can be implemented through Python with Pandas barplot method. For example:

```
import pandas as pd

import seaborn as sns


df = pd.read_csv('SampleData', index_col=0)
```

```
df_grpd = df.groupby("cyl").count().reset_index()

fig = plt.figure(figsize=(12, 8))

sns.barplot(x="cyl", y="mpg", data=df_grpd)
```

Source: https://pythonspot.com/matplotlib-bar-chart/

Pie Chart and Error Bars

Pie charts are created to show proportional data or percentage. Through pie charts, we can summarize huge datasets in visual form and display the relative proportion of different classes of data. On the other hand, error bars are used to show the graphical representation of variability of data and is mainly used to point out errors in data. This approach is also best suited for performing data analysis by overviewing statistical differences between the two groups of data.

Error bars demonstrate how a model and function are used in data analysis. It shows us the variability in data and also indicates any possible errors. To implement these graphs, we can take support from Seaborn Python visualization library. Seaborn provides high level interface for creating attractive statistical graphics and is widely used for visualizing data and plotting. Furthermore, Seaborn provides built in themes for better visualizations and includes built in statistical functions.

Naïve Bayes Model

Naïve Bayes classification theorem is implanted to calculate the probability of data belonging to a specific class. Classification is done by overviewing the previous knowledge about data and is used to solve both binary and multiclass classification problems. Naïve Bayes is a fast and straightforward classification algorithm which is best suitable for large volumes of data. The algorithm has the capability to perform different activities such as text classification, recommender systems, and spam filtering which makes it one of the greatest algorithms used in developing machine learning models.

How is Classification Performed?

To perform classification, data scientists need to understand the given problem and identify datasets to make specific labels. These attributes can also be considered as features of data which are directly affected by labels. Classification is divided into two phases known as evaluation phase and learning phase. In the evaluation phase, the model tests classifier performance on the basis of different parameters including recall, precision, accuracy, and error. For the learning phase, the classifier trains the model on the provided dataset so that it can deliver the best results when implemented in the machine learning system. Computation through Naïve Bayes theorem can be performed by the following equation:

$$P(h|D) = \frac{P(D|h)P(h)}{P(D)}$$

P(h) is the probability of hypothesis h and is also named as the prior probability of h, whereas P(d) is known as the probability of data or prior probability regardless of the hypothesis. P(h|D) is the probability of hypothesis h for given data D and is also named as posterior probability. P(D|h) represents the probability of data d in case of true h hypotheses and is also named as posterior probability.

Naïve Bayes Classified Development in Scikit-Learn

In the below example, we will define the best methods to define dataset, encode features and generate a machine learning model through Python programming language.

Defining the Dataset and Encoding Features to the Data

Basic syntax:

weather=['Sunny','Sunny','Overcast','Rainy','Rainy','Rainy','Overcast','Sunny','Sunny',

'Rainy','Sunny','Overcast','Overcast','Rainy']

temp=['Hot','Hot','Hot','Mild','Cool','Cool','Cool','Mild','Cool','Mild','Mild','Mild','Hot','Mild']

```python
play=['No','No','Yes','Yes','Yes','No','Yes','No','Yes','Yes','Yes','Ye
s','Yes','No']

from sklearn import preprocessing

#creating labelEncoder

le = preprocessing.LabelEncoder()

weather_encoded=le.fit_transform(wheather)

print weather_encoded


Generating model and loading data

from sklearn.naive_bayes import GaussianNB


#Create a Gaussian Classifier

model = GaussianNB()

# Train the model using the training sets

model.fit(features,label)

#Predict Output

predicted= model.predict([[0,2]]) # 0:Overcast, 2:Mild
```

```
print "Predicted Value:", predicted
```

```
#load Data
```

```
from sklearn import datasets
```

```
wine = datasets.load_wine()
```

Implementation of Split() function

```
# Import train_test_split function
```

```
from sklearn.cross_validation import train_test_split
```

```
# Split dataset into training set and test set
```

```
X_train, X_test, y_train, y_test = train_test_split(wine.data,
wine.target, test_size=0.3,random_state=109)
```

Source: https://machinelearningmastery.com/naive-bayes-classifier-scratch-python/

Evaluating Accuracy of the Model

```
from sklearn import metrics
```

```
print("Accuracy:", metrics.accuracy_score(y_test, y_pred))
```

Source:
https://www.datacamp.com/community/tutorials/naive-bayes-scikit-learn

Advantages of Naïve Bayes

Naïve Bayes is a fast approach to obtain accurate model predictions with low computation cost. Furthermore, this theorem can work efficiently on large datasets and performs ideally in case of discrete response variable as compared to continuous variable. As compared to other machine learning models such as logistic regression, Naïve Bayes yields better results in cases of independence holds as well.

K-Means Clustering

The K-Means clustering algorithm is a major part of machine learning algorithms which is based upon three important steps. These steps are named as Initialization, Assignment, and Update. K-Means clustering algorithm is used to partition n observations into k clusters for managing datasets and making accurate predictions in machine learning models.

In the Initialization step, the k means or centroids are generated at random, whereas the Assignment portion allows the creation of k clusters by associating each observation with another nearest centroid. The Update portion allows the centroid of clusters to become new mean and Update and Assignment portions are repeated iteratively until the desired outcome is achieved. As a result, the sum of squared errors is reduced between centroids and their respective points.

To implement K-Means algorithm in Python, we are required to import the following modules at first:

import pandas as pd

import numpy as np

import matplotlib.pyplot as plt

import random

from sklearn import preprocessing

Syntax to read data:

data = pd.read_csv('Sample.csv')

data = data[:30]

max_clusters = 5

data['Age'].fillna(np.mean(data['Age']), inplace = True)

data['Fare'].fillna(np.mean(data['Price']), inplace = True)

data['Age'] = preprocessing.scale(data['Age'])

data['Fare'] = preprocessing.scale(data['Price'])

Expectation-Minimization Algorithm

Expectation-Minimization is an essential part of the K-Means algorithm and it plays a vital role in machine learning model development. This algorithm has the capability to guess cluster centers and repeat the process until the model is fully converged. E-step is used to assign points for nearest cluster center, whereas the M-step is considered to set the clusters to mean. E-step is also known as expectation step because it involves updating of expectations which is used to study point location for each cluster.

Furthermore, the M-step is named as maximization step and it involves maximization of fitness function and is best suited to define the location of cluster centers. In Python programming, there are predefined syntax and libraries to implement K-means algorithm for achieving different outcomes from the machine learning model. K-Means cluster algorithm is limited to linear cluster boundaries which are always linear. In particular, K-means can be implemented in Scikit-Learn through SpectralClustering estimation method for which the following syntax can be used:

from sklearn.cluster import SpectralClustering

model = SpectralClustering(n_clusters=2,
affinity='nearest_neighbors',

```
              assign_labels='kmeans')
```

```
labels = model.fit_predict(X)
```

```
plt.scatter(X[:, 0], X[:, 1], c=labels,
```

```
        s=50, cmap='viridis');
```

Graphical Output:

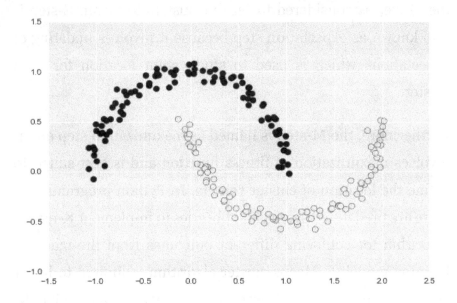

Mean Shift Algorithm

Mean shift algorithm has the capability to assign and outline data points to clusters by turning points towards the mode. This is a hierarchical clustering algorithm based on unsupervised learning techniques and is also named as Mode-seeding algorithm. To apply Mean shift algorithm in Python programming language, we need to perform kernel density estimation and represent the data in mathematical format. This makes it easier for the model to process data and use it for delivering accurate insights and predictions.

Kernel is also known as a function to perform convolution in datasets and is suitable for developing high performing machine learning models. Here is a simple program in Python to demonstrate how Mean shift algorithm works:

```
clusters = [[2, 2, 2], [7, 7, 7], [5, 13, 13]]

X, _ = make_blobs(n_samples = 150, centers = clusters,

                    cluster_std = 0.60)

# After training the model, we store the

coordinates for cluster centers

ms = MeanShift()

ms.fit(X)

cluster_centers = ms.cluster_centers_


# Plot the data points and centroids in 3D graph

fig = plt.figure()

ax = fig.add_subplot(111, projection ='3d')
```

```
ax.scatter(X[:, 0], X[:, 1], X[:, 2], marker ='o')

ax.scatter(cluster_centers[:, 0], cluster_centers[:, 1],

        cluster_centers[:, 2], marker ='x', color ='red',

        s = 300, linewidth = 5, zorder = 10)

plt.show()
```

Output:

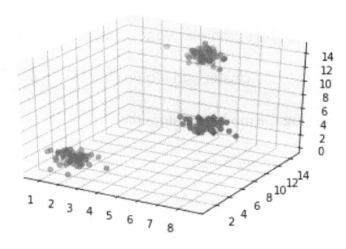

Source: https://www.geeksforgeeks.org/ml-mean-shift-clustering/

There are several advantages of using Mean shift algorithm in machine learning models. The algorithm is good for finding a variable number of modes and is an application independent tool. Furthermore, the model does not assume any prior shape on data clusters like elliptical or spherical.

Chapter 6: Deep Learning and Artificial Intelligence

Machine learning is a branch of computer science which is based on the study of algorithms having the capability to learn and predict on their own. Each algorithm is based on a predefined set of rules and procedures that are used to perform specific operations in machine learning models. These algorithms are also known as Artificial Neural Networks (ANN) in deep learning which is also a subfield of machine learning. Python provides simple and easy to implement approaches for developers and data scientists to program machine learning models and enhance their performance as well.

To develop, maintain, and evaluate deep learning models, we can take help from Python libraries such as Pandas, TensorFlow, and Keras. As they are based on efficient numerical modules, you can get started with deep neural networks and utilize built-in modules to develop high performing machine learning models.

Introduction to Artificial Neural Networks

It is important to learn the basics and functionality of artificial neural networks before starting with deep learning in Python. Neural networks are based on the perception of neurons in the human brain and how they work to perform specific operations. The human brain is the greatest example to be inspired from because it is composed of millions of neurons working together to control different operations in the human body. The brain is capable of performing complex computations within seconds, which is surely the biggest inspiration for artificial neural networks.

Understanding Data

Before developing neural networks or deep learning models, getting information about data and its qualities can deliver long term advantages. At first, check the description folder to overview variables of datasets and learn about details and other vital information as well. Generally, a neural network is comprised of an input layer which is your actual data and is present in numerical form. There are various hidden layers in neural networks which are present between input and output layers. With a single layer, the model is capable of handling linear relationships, whereas in the case of hidden layers, the model can handle non-linear relationships as well.

TensorFlow and Keran are best suited for building multiple layers in a neural network. Here is the syntax to implement these libraries in Python:

pip install tensorflow

import tensorflow.keras as keras

import tensorflow as tf

Once we are done with importing TensorFlow, we can start to prepare our data and make it ready for training in machine learning models. The syntax is defined as follows:

mnist = tf.keras.datasets.mnist

(x_train, y_train),(x_test, y_test) = mnist.load_data()

Keras

To implement Keras, you are required to install and configure Python 2 or 3 along with SciPy and NumPy libraries. TensorFlow and Keras can be installed and configured without complex coding because there are predefined Python modules which you can easily add in your program.

Starting with the first step, we need to load our dataset for which the following two classes form Keras library can be implemented to define the model:

from numpy import loadtxt

from keras.models import sequential

from keras.layers import Dense

Source: https://machinelearningmastery.com/keras-functional-api-deep-learning/

Defining Keras Model

To define Keras model, we need to develop a sequential model and add layers until the required network architecture is complete. There are specific heuristics to determine the best network structure for which data scientists implement the process of trial and error experimentation. A fully connected layer can be defined by Dense class and we can also specify the number of nodes or neurons present in the layer by the help of activation argument. Python syntax to define Keras model is defined as follows:

model = Sequential()

model.add(Dense(10, input_dim=5, activation= 'relu'))

model.compile(loss- 'binary_crossentropy' , optimizer = 'adam', metrics= ['accuracy'])

Evaluation and Prediction

For evaluating Keras model, we can use the evaluate() function on the model and pass the same input and output for training as well. Moreover, this activity will also generate a prediction for every input and output including the average loss or accuracy metrics. Implementation in Python for evaluating the model and predicting values in Keras is defined as follows:

accuracy = model.evaluate(X, y)

```
print('Accuracy: %.2f %(accuracy*100))

predictions = model.predict(X)

predictions = model.predict_classes(X)
```

Machine Learning

Machine learning is a branch of Artificial Intelligence which is based on statistical methods and cognitive behavior. The concept also allows computers to learn on their own without being programmed repeatedly whenever the system is exposed to new data. The process of prediction and training is based on specialized algorithms which are developed to perform specific tasks in machine learning models. For developing machine learning systems in Python programming language, major libraries including SciPy, NumPy, Matplotlib, Pandas, Keran and Scikit-learn need to be installed and configured at first.

For efficient learning and accurate predictions, machine learning models should be fed with data having certain attributes and variables during training. Majorly, machine learning tasks are categorized as predictive modeling, clustering, and concept learning whereas the ultimate goal of developing ML models is to take decisions without human intervention.

Categories of Machine Learning

Machine learning is divided into three main sections: Supervised learning, Unsupervised learning, and Reinforcement learning. Supervised learning is the most used paradigm for building machine learning models because it is absolutely easy to understand and implement. With the passage of time, ML models become capable of learning the relationship between examples and their labels until they become fully trained to make accurate predictions.

Supervised and Unsupervised Learning

Supervised learning algorithms have the power to model relationships and dependencies to achieve specific target prediction output. Common algorithms for implementing supervised learning are Nearest neighbor, Decision Trees, Naïve Bayes, and Neural networks. Unsupervised learning is based on machine learning models that are trained with unlabeled data. The models are not given any supporting training datasets and they have to learn through patterns and attributes in data. Common algorithms for developing unsupervised machine learning models are K-Means clustering and Association Rules. Unsupervised learning algorithms are mainly used in the development of descriptive modeling and pattern detection systems because there are no labels or output categories defined.

Another major category of machine learning is named as Semi-supervising learning. For supervised and unsupervised machine learning models, there are labels for data given in some cases whereas in other scenarios, there are no labels for observation in datasets. Categories and techniques of machine learning are selected after complete observation and evaluation of external factors such as cost, security, reliability, and maintenance. These factors play a vital role in machine learning model development as well.

Reinforcement Learning

The reinforcement learning method has a capability to utilize observations from interaction with external factors and environments to make specific decisions in a machine learning model. Agents in reinforcement learning models consistently learn from the environment and repeatedly try for exploring a new range of possible states. Being an important part of machine learning and artificial intelligence, reinforcement learning allows systems and software agents to automatically determine ideal behavior within a certain context to boost performance.

There are several algorithms to implement the reinforcement learning model in Python. Usually, reinforcement learning models are created for a specific problem and all of the solutions are given by the model itself. Common algorithms for reinforcement learning are Q-Learning, Deep Adversarial Networks, and Temporal Difference.

Deep Neural Networks

What are Neural Networks?

Deep neural networks are comprised of various algorithms which are modeled according to the functionality and connectivity of the human brain to recognize specific patterns. The human brain has the capability to predict, analyze, and make decisions overviewing any given scenarios and perform tasks successfully. Neural networks classify and cluster data and utilize the given variables and attributes to make relevant predictions and perform certain tasks as well. A deep neural network is actually a neural network with a certain level of complexity because it is based on more than two layers.

By using mathematical modeling, neural networks process data in different ways because they are designed to simulate the activity of the human brain. Furthermore, the model performs specific types of ordering and sorting by utilizing artificial intelligence and machine learning approaches. Patterns recognized by neural networks are numerical and include vectors through which any real-world data such as sound, time series, or text could be translated. Moreover, they also group unlabeled data as per its similarities when provided a labeled dataset.

Neural networks are comprised of various components. These include an input layer, an output layer, and some hidden layers as well. To complete the network architecture, we can select an activation function for each hidden layer along with a set of biases and weights between the layers. We can easily create a neural network in Python through the following syntax:

```python
class NeuralNetwork:

    def __init__(self, x, y):

    self.input      = x

    self.weights1  = np.random.rand(self.input.shape[2],8)

    self.weights2  = np.random.rand(4,1)

        self.y         = y

    self.output    = np.zeros(y.shape)
```

Generally, the values for biases and weights determine the strength and effectiveness of predictions. Training of neural networks involves fine tuning of biases and weights from input data for which we are required to perform different iterations. Each iteration of training involves the calculation of feed forward and updating of biases and weights through back propagation approach.

Recurrent Neural Networks

Recurrent Neural Networks are also known as RNNs and are basically used in the implementation of Natural Language Processing or language modeling because they allow data to flow in any direction. As they can repeat the same task for each element of the sequence, the output is usually dependent on the previous computations and RNNs are known to have built-in memory that records the previously calculated information.

Training Neural Networks

Training neural networks is an essential part of machine learning model development. As we are required to find the most suitable values of weights and bias of a neural network to achieve the desired output, the training must be performed by using effective techniques such as the iterative gradient descent method. Once random initialization is complete, we can make predictions on subset of data through forward propagation process and update each weight by an amount proportional to dC/dq or the derivative of cost functions with respect to the weight. The calculation can also be referred to as the learning rate and implemented through a computational graph as well. Gradients can be calculated through back-propagation algorithm for which we can implement chain rule of differentiation as well.

Back propagation algorithm is implemented by analyzing data through a computational graph which has each neuron expanded to several nodes. The computational graph does not have any kind of bias or weights on the edges, so weights become their own nodes.

Gradient Descent

Gradient descent optimization technique is used to find out which weight produces the fewest errors and is used to translate signals from input data into a correct classification. A neural network learns and adjusts to several weights so that it can map signal meaning in the best suitable manner. Furthermore, each weight factor in deep network is based on several transforms because the signal of weight has to pass through different sums and activation over the layers. The idea behind deep learning is to adjust a model's weight and increase its performance and capability to make accurate predictions.

Deep learning can process millions of images and classify them as per their similarities. As it performs automatic feature extraction, we can perform complex tasks without human intervention even by training machine learning models on unlabeled data. During processing, neural networks try to learn and recognize correlations between the features and optimal results. This activity is done by drawing specific connections between feature signals and labeled data.

Optimization

The training process of deep learning neural networks is dependent upon input data, labels, and attributes. As they learn to map inputs and outputs over a training dataset of examples, the process is usually iterative and involves finding a set of weights that are best suited for the network. An iterative training process for neural networks is best for solving optimization problem and searches for model weights that yield minimum loss or error when evaluation examples in training datasets. Remember that optimization is a search procedure and can become challenging when implemented in deep neural network models.

To perform optimization and training for deep learning neural networks, the best method is back propagation of the error algorithm. Generally, we can handle the difficulty in terms of features of error surface or landscape which the algorithm has undergone changes so that it can navigate on its own and select the right path as well.

Artificial Neural Networks

The Artificial Neural Networks are based on the working and functionality of biological neural networks and are capable of modeling non linear relationships between inputs and outputs. Being statistical models, Artificial neural networks are widely implemented in machine learning systems because they are based on the approach of learning and observing datasets. Optimization techniques such as cost function allow ANN's to determine best values of each tunable model parameter and improve the learning rate as well. Furthermore, these optimization techniques allow developers and data scientists to develop state of the art machine learning models which are capable of making accurate predictions and insights.

Machine learning models are complex because of the increased abstraction and higher problem-solving capabilities. Due to the increased number of hidden layers, the number of paths between each neuron and given layer increases which in return makes the ANN system more complex. Tuning and model architecture are major components of Artificial Neural Networks. Each of these characteristics allow ANN to make a significant impact on the reliability and performance of the deep learning model.

Remember the fact that Artificial Neural Networks are extremely powerful and they can often become complex. Furthermore, they are also named as black box algorithms as their actual working and functionality is impossible to understand. In contrast with deep learning algorithms, these models are also dependent on optimal model selection and model tuning approach for maximizing performance and output. Furthermore, statistical techniques and deep learning leverage concepts are a major part of Artificial Neural Networks.

How Do They Work?

Artificial Neural Networks have the capability to make decisions and calculations on their own. As the model works as a supervised learning approach, it is fed with enough examples and similar scenarios which allow ANN's to make accurate predictions on their own. This process is usually done through back propagation approach because Artificial Neural Networks are represented as weighted directed graphs. In these graphs, node is designed by artificial neurons for which the connection between neuron inputs and neuron outputs is represented through directed edges and weights.

Each given input is multiplied with its corresponding weights and the output is directly dependent upon the details and labels of the weight for solving a specific problem. Furthermore, the weights are represented through the strength of interconnection in between neurons of the artificial neural network. In case the weighted sum is zero, we can add a bias to make output non-zero or update the system to meet the model's requirements. Weights of inputs can range from zero to positive infinity and to keep the response according to the limits of desired values, we can create a specific threshold value as well.

Furthermore, activation functions can also be implemented in artificial neural networks which comprise of a set of functions implemented to achieve a desired value. Some of the common activation functions are named as Sigmoidal, Tan hyperbolic sigmoidal, and binary.

Architecture of ANN's

Artificial Neural Networks or ANN's contain a huge number of artificial neurons, and this is the main reason they are named as artificial neural networks. The architecture is comprised of an Input layer, an Output layer, and a Hidden layer. The input layer has artificial neurons which are subject to receive input from external resources and are responsible for learning and recognition as well. For the output layer, the information that is fed into the system is analyzed and recognized before it is sent for further processing. Moreover, the output layer also accepts or rejects the training data by overviewing the labels and attributes to make sure that the information is best suited for the artificial neural network. The illustration below will better help you in understanding the architecture of artificial neural networks:

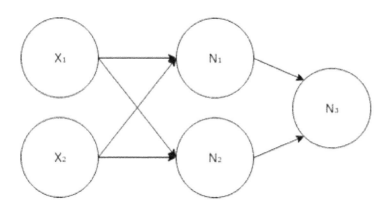

Hidden layers are present between input layers and output layers. Their job is to transform the input into meaningful data so that the output layer can utilize it in the best manner. Each of the artificial neural networks is interconnected and the hidden layers cover each portion of data present in the system. This makes it easier to complete the learning process and allows the system to make relevant updates without any hassle.

Advantages

Artificial neural networks have several key advantages that make them ideal for solving complex problems in machine learning and artificial intelligence. Having the capability to model non-linear relationships, ANNs can solve real life problems by defining relationships between inputs and outputs from non linear data as well. Furthermore, artificial neural networks can learn from initial inputs and generalize relationships to predict unseen data and make the model capable of performing complex operations without any hassle. Unlike other prediction models, artificial neural networks never impose any restrictions over input variables which allows researchers to train the model through different techniques.

Applications of ANNs

Character recognition and image processing are the greatest applications of artificial neural networks. As this network has the power to process large sets of input data, it can also define non-linear relationships and help in the development of character and image recognition applications. Artificial neural network models are widely implemented in fraud detection and security systems because they have the capability to perform facial recognition in real time.

Moreover, artificial neural networks also serve as a useful tool for food quality and safety analysis. This covers the development of microbial growth models through which prediction of food safety and interpretation of spectroscopic data is performed.

Chapter 7: Data Science in Real World

Data science is a combination of statistics, mathematics, and programming. In order to develop data science and machine learning models, we are required to have in depth knowledge and information regarding the subject so that accurate training data can be fed into the system. On the other hand, business thinking and domain knowledge are also essential for developing high performing machine learning models and data science projects.

Python is a completely suitable programming language for developing machine learning and data science models because it is absolutely easy to learn and implement. Furthermore, we can perform specific tasks and operations by utilizing built-in Python libraries such as Pandas, NumPy and Scikit-Learn.

How Can We Implement Data Science in Real Life Scenarios?

Most industries and businesses are now using systems that are based on the latest machine learning and data science models. This helps in automating processes and allows businesses to make accurate predictions for the future to increase sales and boost profits. Traditional information systems are not capable of bringing long term benefits to companies and businesses because of outdated technology. To make things better, data scientists and machine learning experts have utilized the concepts of computer science, mathematics, and statistics to develop systems which are capable of making accurate predictions and learn from the training datasets as well.

There are several key advantages of data science in business and real life for humans. An experienced data scientist can also serve as a trusted advisor and strategic partner to the company by providing accurate data insights and predictions for the future. This activity is done through measuring performance across the entire organization and recording performance metrics. Furthermore, data scientists perform different tests to determine the status of an organization's current analytics system to bring further improvements.

Data Science Applications

Most of the advanced applications and systems developed nowadays are based on machine learning and data science models. The impact and performance of machine learning systems is a lot better as compared to traditional computing systems which is the main reason why machine learning and artificial intelligence are widely being researched. By using data science, companies and businesses have become intelligent enough to sell products and promote their services in a shorter time frame.

Here are a few major applications of Data Science:

Image recognition

You might have noticed that once you have uploaded any image with your friends on Facebook, you start to get suggestions for adding tags. This feature of automatic suggestion is based on an image recognition algorithm which has the capability to detect specific patterns and yield outcomes with matching data. Furthermore, image recognition systems are widely being used by security agencies and financial institutes to detect people involved in fraudulent activities in real time.

Speech Recognition

Speech recognition systems allow users to perform different tasks by communicating with their devices such as smartphones or computers. Google Voice, Cortana, and Siri are the finest implementations of speech recognition systems that were originally designed with machine learning and data science models.

Virtual Assistants

Chatbots from different websites and applications are the finest implementation of deep learning and artificial intelligence. Virtual assistance is now available in mobile applications through which patients can avail healthcare guidance and basic support without any hassle. Furthermore, you can book appointments and make schedules with chatbots through virtual assistants and receive vital information as well.

Risk and Fraud Detection

Financial institutions such as banks are the biggest users of automated fraud detection and risk management systems. Banks can now analyze user data and information to check credit history for thousands of people instead of checking for everyone individually. Furthermore, companies can avoid bad debts and losses by overviewing and managing transactions in real time.

Data Analytics in Detail

Data analytics is an approach which is used to analyze data sets and draw conclusions regarding the available data. To tackle the increasing demand and requirements of businesses and companies, research for specialized software and systems is being performed by data scientists and machine learning engineers to improve scientific models and theories. Online analytical processing and business intelligence are the major forms of advanced analytics. Data analytics systems can make businesses improve operational efficiency and increase revenue by meeting customer demands and increasing sales.

Analyzing and evaluating data are the basic concepts of data analytics. Most of the work in the development of data analytics systems includes collection, integration, and preparation of data which has to be used for model training. The models are then tested and upgraded to produce accurate results. For development of data analytics models, the first step is data collection for which scientists take support from particular analytics applications and work with data engineers to implement the information in the best possible manner.

Data combined from different sources needs to be refined with data integration tools so that it can be transformed into a common format. Once the labels and format are properly analyzed, we can load the data into an analytics system such as Datawarehouse or Hadoop cluster for fast processing. Moreover, data scientists have to find and solve data quality problems so that the accuracy of analytics applications is never compromised. Furthermore, data cleansing and data profiling techniques can be used to make sure that the data set is consistent and free of mistakes. This will help in achieving accurate insights and predictions in future.

Analytical models are built by taking support from predictive modeling tools and programming languages such as Python or Scala. Once the model is developed, it undergoes proper testing for which different types of test training datasets are used. The process is repeated until the model completely learns and adapts characteristics from training data so that it can make accurate predictions when implemented into the system. Furthermore, the model is also run in production mode for which full datasets are used and if any problem arises, it is solved immediately to ensure reliability and performance of the analytics model.

Types and Categories of Data Analytics

Generally, data analytics is divided into four major categories which are predictive, prescriptive, diagnostic, and descriptive analysis. Each of the categories has unique characteristics and is capable of performing various operations for business analytic models. Starting with predictive analysis, the category is best for gaining insights and predictions for the future. This approach uses historical data to identify the given records and trends which are likely to occur. Furthermore, predictive analysis tools also provide valuable insights for scenarios which might happen in the future if they are likely to occur. To implement predictive analysis, we can use machine learning techniques including decision trees, regression, and neural networks.

Prescriptive analysis approach gives us ideas for activities that could be performed to avail best outcomes. The technique uses insights from predictive analysis to make reliable data driven decisions. Furthermore, businesses can get help from predictive analysis to determine the likelihood of events and outcomes because this approach has the capability to detect patterns in large datasets. Diagnostic analytics can be helpful for obtaining reasons related to the happening of certain aspects in an analytics model. The technique takes points from descriptive analysis and works deeper to find the root cause of each event.

Moreover, diagnostic analysis also includes performance indicators which help to discover the main reason which might have affected the performance or reliability of the analytics system. Diagnostic analysis is used to identify and outline anomalies in data and information related to each anomaly is also collected. At the end, data scientists implement statistical techniques to find trends and relationships to outline the root causes of these anomalies. The fourth category of data analytics is named as descriptive analysis which summarizes large datasets into separate portions for describing outcomes in a better way.

Descriptive analysis can be considered as a way of analyzing the main reason why a specific scenario happened for which data scientists implement key performance indicators (KPI) to develop analytics models. Furthermore, other metrics like return on investment (ROI) are also based on descriptive analysis because they are implemented in systems for large scale businesses and industries to gain performance and sales insights.

Importance of Data Analytics

Analyzing big data is an essential part of machine learning model development. There is a wide range of applications of data analytics that have greatly improved the performance of business systems and have allowed companies to compete in today's world. Talking about the earliest adopters of data analytics tools, the financial sector has widely implemented machine learning and data analytics systems to secure transactions and avoid fraudulent activities. Furthermore, data analytics can also be used to detect fraud in real time and take certain actions to stop all kinds of fraudulent activities.

Data analytic also provides vital information for healthcare, environment protection, and crime prevention. These applications bring long term advantages and support for people as they can protect themselves from fraudulent activities and get medical assistance without any hassle. Data analysis, statistics, and mathematics have always been a part of scientific research through which advanced analytic techniques and tools are designed. The Internet of Things (IoT) is another great invention made through data analytics methods and its devices are comprised of sensors that collect meaningful data which is then utilized by data analytics models to make predictions and accurate insights. There are endless applications of data analytics and the increasing volume of data being collected each day reveals new pathways for machine learning and deep analytics models to learn effectively.

Data Mining

This is the method of analyzing data from various perspectives and converting it into useful information. The converted and summarized information is used to make vital decisions and training data. In machine learning models, data mining is considered as a technique of detecting, analyzing, and exploring patterns in large amounts of data and the processed information is then sorted and classified into separate categories. Moreover, classification and data prediction techniques help us in getting accurate insights and prediction results through data mining methods without any hassle.

Logistic regression, classification trees, neural networks, anomaly detection, and clustering techniques such as K-nearest Neighbors are a few examples of data mining. The characteristics of data analysis are dependent upon different aspects such as variety, velocity, and volume. In order to get better results and outcomes from data mining, we are required to address each scenario in-depth and implement the best algorithms to develop data mining models. Furthermore, framing a problem makes data scientist clear about the requirements of systems and helps data scientists to gain accurate insights from the data mining model.

Steps in Data Mining

The first step in data mining is data cleaning, in which we are supposed to check the quality of data and remove any kind of irregularities. Multiple data sources are combined to complete the data integration process so that data could be extracted from the database. Data selection and data transformation approaches are used to perform summary analysis and aggregatory operations over data while doing data mining. In data mining, we have to extract useful information and data from the data source and analyze several patterns as well.

In the final step of knowledge representation, data scientists have to represent knowledge to users in the form of metrics, graphs, trees, and tables. Data mining is widely implemented in the development of fraud detection, risk management, market analysis, and corporate analysis systems to explore and manage data.

Importance of Machine Learning

Machine learning is responsible for transforming operations for each sector including finance, health care, security, information technology, and education. Based on the idea of learning from data, machine learning is a branch of artificial intelligence that automates analytical model building and allows systems to make decisions without human intervention. Because of the ever-increasing advancements and revolutions in computing technologies, businesses can find the best solutions to boost their sales and increase profits.

The aim of machine learning is to understand the structure of data and utilize theoretical models for developing systems which are capable of making accurate predictions and data insights. Data driven decisions always bring positive outcomes for businesses because machine learning models are trained on factual data which delivers the best possible solutions for any problem. In traditional computing systems, data analysis was performed through trial and error-based approach which cannot yield accurate results when implemented over large data sets and heterogeneous data.

Data Science Lifecycle and Model Building

Building data science models by focusing on each important aspect of the data science lifecycle will help you in achieving the best results and outcomes. Discovery, data preparation, model planning, model building, operations, and results analysis are key portions of the data science lifecycle. Starting with the first steps of discovery and data preparation, data scientists need to understand the requirements, specifications, and priorities of the system. Budget and time constraints should also be kept in mind before starting the project, as it will save you from further issues as well.

In the data preparation phase, sufficient training data and information must be discovered so that the data science model is capable of making accurate predictions and evaluations in future. Extract, transform, and load are the major approaches that should be considered while creating datasets for the system. Once the data preparation step is done, the next part is model planning where data scientists have to determine the techniques and methods to draw relationships between variables.

The next phase is known as model building in which data scientists and engineers have to develop datasets for testing and training purposes. Implementing techniques like clustering, association, and classification will make it easier to complete the model building phase. For the operations phase, data scientists are supposed to deliver briefings, technical documents, code, and final reports for the project.

Challenges in Neural Networks and Deep Learning Algorithms

Neural networks and deep learning algorithms are widely used in the development of machine learning and artificial intelligence models. Although the performance and effectiveness of deep learning models is directly dependent upon the quality and reliability of training data, there are several other factors that can be held accountable for the performance of machine learning models. Overfitting and underfitting are two of the major challenges that are faced by ML systems and to prevent further loss, data scientists have to research and implement effective techniques to improve the performance and functionality of machine learning models.

To avoid overfitting, we can apply regularization methods such as data augmentation, drop out, early stopping, and transfer learning during training of deep learning models. This will help in protecting the model from overfitting and also improves rare dependencies. For neural networks, we use the dropout approach which is a popular regularization technique to finish overfitting. Other methods like early stopping, data augmentation, and transfer learning can also be implemented to avoid the challenges that are being faced during the development of deep learning and neural network systems.

Deep Learning Limitations

Although deep learning systems are great performers, there are some external factors which can have a direct impact on their functionality and effectiveness. Usually, artificial intelligence models are given training through a supervised learning approach which includes training data that is completely labeled and classified by humans. Deep learning systems are based on the same approach and require huge training datasets to become properly trained. Complex and large models are difficult to train for which data scientists need to classify and label training data as well.

Improving Data Science Models

Machine learning models developed with the Python programming language can be updated and improved by making simple changes in the code. Although there are different checks to overview the performance and effectiveness of a data science model, we need to focus on some key factors explained below to avail best outcomes:

Determine Problems

For improving results, we need to analyze the problems with our data science model at first. Learning curves are a great source to verify a test set against the provided training data. By analyzing computational graphs, one can easily identify the weaknesses of a data analytics or machine learning model. Furthermore, you can also perform cross validation to overview performance of your model. A large difference between the results and cross validation estimates is a common problem which usually occurs with training data.

Choosing Hyper Parameters

When solving a data science problem, you need to analyze the problem and determine the best metric for getting a long-term solution. Remember that most of the algorithms perform best even with default parameter settings. However, you can optimize the efficiency of machine learning and artificial intelligence models by implementing hyperparameters as well. To perform this activity, you have to design a grid search containing possible values supported by your parameters and start to evaluate the results through a score metric.

Testing and Evaluation

Testing and evaluation will help you in determining the quality of predictions and data insights delivered by a deep analytics model. In some cases, bias can affect the performance of the model for which you can implement various techniques such as automatic feature creation and support vectors to achieve a better solution. Although these techniques will make the model perform slightly better, your understanding and expertise regarding the machine learning model are the best source to examine, test, and improve the overall performance and efficiency.

Search for More Data

No matter what amount of training data you have used, there is always room for improvement because machine learning and deep learning models always improve when a new data set is fed into the system. Increasing the size of the training set is also a vital approach to be considered. In case you have been training your model with simple data, you can feed complex or unlabeled data so that the model is capable of learning and making better decisions on its own.

Chapter 8: Deep Learning and Business

Business processes nowadays are completely transformed due to the involvement of artificial intelligence, deep learning, and machine learning systems. They are key aspects of enacting digital transformation and development of computational systems. There are several forms of prescriptive analysis that can help businesses in achieving desired outcomes within a short period of time. These procedures include automated stock transactions, intelligent traffic flow pattern optimization, autonomous data center functions, and autonomous cars. The basic fundamentals behind each of these technologies are deep learning and major concepts of artificial intelligence.

Actually, artificial intelligence is an approach to mimic human intelligence process through the application of mathematical and statistical algorithms. Machine learning is actually a subset of artificial intelligence and is a major field of computer science that focuses on interpreting structures and patterns in data.

How Does Deep Learning Work?

Deep learning is an approach based on the construct of human neural networks and is also a subfield of machine learning and artificial intelligence. The approach has the capability to learn from both structured and unstructured data to initiate automated learning from training data. In order to improve accuracy of deep learning models, data scientists need to remove weak correlations and assumptions in data. The presence of reliable and high-quality data is the key aspect to building accurate machine learning models.

For extracting more information from existing data, we can follow the feature engineering approach in deep learning. This method is used to extract new facilities and features from data and allows the deep learning model to understand variance in data as well. As a result, data scientists are able to develop models with improved accuracy and better prediction capabilities. Feature engineering is based on a hypothesis generation approach which is divided into feature transformation and feature creation methods.

In feature transformation, the algorithms work with normally distributed data. Methods such as inverse, square root, or log of the values are implemented to remove skewness from data and this approach is also known as data normalization. Numeric data can also be created by adding discrete values into the deep learning model. On the other hand, feature creation method derives new variables from existing variables and helps to uncover hidden relationships between datasets. Moreover, data scientists also take support from the feature selection process to find out the best subset of attributes to explain the relationship of independent variables with the available target variable.

Feature selection is based on major machine learning model development metrics like domain knowledge and visualization. Through domain knowledge, we can select features which might yield a higher impact on target variable whereas the visualization approach helps to visualize the relationship between multiple variables. In return, this approach makes variable selection processes easier and more effective. To enhance performance and reliability of the model, we can also consider working on statistical parameters like p-values and other modules to select the right features.

Algorithm Tuning and Method Ensemble

The performance of machine learning algorithms is dependent upon parameters and variables in the dataset. The parameters can influence the efficiency and outcome of the learning process for which data scientists follow the approach of algorithm tuning. This approach is used to figure out the best value for each parameter which in return improves the accuracy of the model. To tune the parameters, you should have in-depth knowledge about the machine learning model and datasets in advance. Furthermore, the process can be repeated multiple times until the desired outcome is achieved.

Ensemble methods are commonly used in the development and maintenance of machine learning and deep learning models. This technique combines outcomes of weak models and performs operations to produce a model with better results. Bagging and boosting are two major techniques used to implement ensemble methods on machine learning models.

Model Interpretability

Businesses and industries require information systems that have the capability to deliver accurate data insights and predictions that bring long term benefits to the organization. To deliver the best machine learning models in industry, we need to interpret and analyze the effectiveness and performance of deep learning and artificial intelligence models before starting with the implementation process. Model interpretability in machine learning is an approach which is used to assess how easy it is for humans to evaluate and understand the working process of a machine learning model.

Models such as logistic regression are ideal for use in the development of business AI models because you can add extra features and implement deep learning methods to meet system requirements. Model interpretability is immensely important because algorithm outcomes are responsible for making high stakes decisions and it is mandatory to know which features to add and which need to be removed. Additionally, in case the model is not interpretable, the company might not be legally permitted to make changes to processes by using insights.

Model interpretability can be performed with the help of DataRobot. DataRobot features several components that yield fully human-interpretable models because of the model blueprint and feature explanation techniques. Model blueprint provides insights related to the preprocessing steps on which each model is based to achieve a desired outcome. Furthermore, it also helps data scientists to justify the models and explain regulatory details if needed.

On the other hand, prediction explanations reveal the top variables that can make an impact on the model's outcome. This allows users to explain how the model has derived a specific outcome and the steps involved in deriving accurate predictions and data insights.

Deep Learning in Business Systems

Pioneers in deep learning system development have been using artificial intelligence and deep learning to advance machine learning model capabilities. These advancements have deployed at scale in order to achieve greater efficiency and speed for which a wide range of new training data is used in model training. Business systems now require deep learning models that are capable of making real time decisions and deliver outcomes that bring long term benefits to the business. The process of scoring predictive models and processing of decision requests in real time have added great value to machine learning models.

Technologies today have advanced to a point where machine learning models can be implemented and deployed at a scale to achieve better performance, reliability, and effectiveness. These advances are unleashing new pathways of data science capabilities such as the acceptance of real time decision requests from various channels and processing of decision requests in real time according to the given business rules. To handle thousands of requests per second, machine learning engineers have to design and control processes through multiple model recalibration methods.

Usage of Deep Learning in Businesses and Industries

Marketing, Sales, and Finance industries are the biggest users of deep learning models and machine learning algorithms. Modern day marketing models and approaches are designed to attract customers and improve sales by showcasing services of a company in unique ways. To make this happen, marketing departments work to find large datasets which are then implemented in deep learning models to understand customer purchase decisions and recommendations. Deep learning has the power to replace traditional heuristics-based lead scoring because it can determine relationships between data and generate useful insights as well. On the other hand, sales teams can also get support from deep learning models to analyze customer predictions.

Generally, companies and businesses get unstructured data from a variety of sources and sales teams are unable to understand purchasing trends of customers. With the help of deep learning models, businesses are now able to predict insights, deal cycles, and deal sizes which can yield the highest return on investment and sales ratio. Evaluating customer and sales interactions that are likely to yield best outcomes can deliver long term benefits to business for which deep learning models are ideal and best performing.

In the finance sector, we can see deep learning and artificial intelligence systems that are used to perform certain tasks to avoid fraud and analyze credit history of customers. Banks can now overview credit history for thousands of customers within seconds and make major decisions such as loan approval with the help of automated machine learning systems. Furthermore, machine learning systems have also eliminated the need to perform manual data entry for which predictive modeling algorithms and machine learning methods are used.

Applications

Here are some examples of the best deep learning applications that have brought significant benefits and ease to humans.

Language Recognition

Language recognition systems are based on deep learning models which allows them to differentiate dialects of any language. The dialects are determined by artificial intelligence models and can be differentiated in real time without human involvement. Language recognition and translation systems are some of the best implementations of deep learning algorithms as they can perform translation from images and text in real time as well.

Autonomous Vehicles

The biggest revolution in our transport system is the addition of self-driving or autonomous vehicles. Artificial intelligence and machine learning models in self-driving vehicles have the capability to detect patterns, humans, and other traffic for making accurate decisions.

Computer Vision and Text Generation

The deep learning approach has provided best models for image classification, image segmentation, and object detection systems. Computer vision and text generation methods are widely used in education systems because they have the capability to automate tasks and perform required text generation without any hassle.

Limitations of Machine Learning Models

Machine learning models developed with Python and R programming languages are capable of automating processing and deliver accurate insights when trained through high quality training datasets. It is simple to understand the value of ML and the great advantages it has brought in today's world. Although technology has greatly revolutionized how different tasks and processes are done, there are still a lot of limitations and consequences of automating tasks which need to be overlooked by human beings.

Information explosion has now resulted in the collection of massive amounts of data, and this amount of data is engaged with rapid development of computer parallelization and processor power. The concept of trusting machine learning models has its own advantages and disadvantages. When trained with high quality training data, artificial intelligence and machine learning systems can generate 100 percent accurate predictions and complete the given tasks without failure. Although machines can never achieve the level of human intelligence, they have significantly improved with time to bring positive outcomes.

Machine learning models can never tell us about the normative values which need to be accepted and answers to questions like how we should act in certain scenarios. The approach is extremely powerful for sensors and can be used to design and calibrate systems for delivering accurate outcomes.

Finding Useful Data

The most vital part of developing and training a deep learning model is to find accurate and high-quality data. If you feed a model with poor or unstructured data, it will surely provide inaccurate results in future. Finding quality data is difficult for which data scientists need to verify the resources and include information that is completely reliable and authentic. Furthermore, most of the machine learning models require huge amounts of data to be trained perfectly. The larger the architecture, the greater the size of data needed to produce viable results.

Reusing data in machine learning models is surely a bad approach. In case you are not able to find data in bulk, try to train your model with labeled and structured data so that it can learn within a short period of time. Whenever fake data is fed into a machine learning model, it will start to train by itself and when tested on an unseen data set, it might not deliver accurate prediction results. Like quality of training data, features also play a vital role in the predictions made by machine learning models.

Chapter 9: Advanced Python Data Science

Data is the core part of the machine learning model development process. Traditional data and Big Data are major types of data that are used to train machine learning models. It has become mandatory to build new platforms to meet the ever-increasing demand of organizations. There are several challenges and difficulties faced by traditional data because it requires collaborative efforts of people to be managed and utilizes a lot of resources and time as well.

What is Big Data?

Big data is known as the collection of large amounts of information which is processed and manipulated for analytics. This approach is divided into three major portions which are volume, velocity, and variety. In the volume section, organizations have to collect information and data from different sources including social media, industrial equipment, Internet, and business transactions. Storage mediums like Hadoop and Data lakes are widely used to store and process information in big data.

To deal with millions of transactions each minute, big data systems have built in velocity handling modules. Moreover, data streams and tons of information from the Internet can now be processed through big data algorithms without any hassle. Data is present in different formats; it can be either structured or unstructured for which the variety properties in big data are used to handle database operations.

Importance of Big Data

Big data systems can change the way we handle information. When it comes to handling large volumes of data, we need to select the most suitable tools and models to manage the available information. With the implementation of big data, companies can take data from any source and manipulate it to get accurate insights. Tools such as in-memory analytics and Hadoop can identify new sources of data and reduce the time needed to process the information. Furthermore, these tools are cost saving and can help companies in processing large volumes of data without any hassle.

There is no business that claims success without having the need to develop strong customer relations. Customers are the most vital asset for any business and if the company is not able to deliver quality services, losing potential customers becomes inevitable. The use of big data systems allows businesses to analyze customer behavior and purchase decisions by overviewing the trends and patterns in data.

Organizational Benefits

Advanced Python data science applications are designed to bring long term benefit to large scale industries and businesses. Big data systems help businesses to understand market trends, evaluate product effectiveness, and gain information regarding customer behavior. Furthermore, the approach also promotes cost saving measures and delivers high returns and meaningful insights within a short period of time. Machine learning and artificial intelligence systems have to handle big data regularly for which the model is programmed to learn and gain insights from high quality data. In return, this approach brings long term benefit to companies and businesses.

Modern day computing systems provide the power, flexibility, and speed needed to access huge amounts of big data. Furthermore, companies need new methods with reliable access and storage facilities in order to store and manage huge volumes of data. High performance tools such as in-memory analytics and grid computing have greatly increased reliability and efficiency of big data systems.

Python Machine Learning Limitations

Python is the finest general purpose and high-level programming language which is widely being used by developers to create state of the art machine learning and artificial intelligence models. Compilation of a Python program is not similar to a conventional C or C++ program because its execution occurs with the support of an interpreter. For other languages, the compiler is responsible for executing and running the program. This makes Python execution slower as compared to the execution of other programming languages. Furthermore, memory consumption of Python is higher because of the complexity of data types and implementation of libraries.

There are specific limitations of Python programming language which make it difficult for beginners to develop machine learning models through Python. Numerous kinds of runtime errors occur during the development of Python programs which need to be addressed sequentially to avoid any future problems. Moreover, Python features and extensions can be customized to make programming easier, as this is not the case with other programming languages such as C, C++ and R.

Reasons to select Python in Data Science

Python programming language allows programmers to express logical concepts and libraries without writing long lines of code.

There are no extra steps to compile and execute steps as we can directly run the program through source code. Furthermore, Python has the capability to convert the source code into bytecodes so that it can be easily translated into the native language of the computer. Developers can load and link libraries directly without adding any type of additional lines of code or functions.

Memory management and exception handling approaches make Python suitable for developing data analytics and machine learning models. Python standard libraries including Pandas, NumPy, and Matplotlib are the ultimate sources to design, develop and test machine learning models. Libraries provide pre-written piece of code which can be enhanced by the developers to meet the requirements of the machine learning model. As machine learning requires continuous data processing, Python libraries can be used to access, handle, and transform data without any hassle.

For handling basic machine learning algorithms such as linear regression, clustering and classification, we can use Scikit-Learn library whereas Pandas library is best for handling high level data structures. Pandas allows data scientists to gather data from external sources and also performs filtration of information to create high quality training datasets. Moreover, Pandas also provides extra facilities such as data extraction from external resources such as Excel.

Is Machine Learning Perfect?

Despite its amazing advantages and facilities in the real world, machine learning models cannot be considered one hundred percent perfect and ideal. Although data scientists and machine learning engineers are researching to make AI models work accurately and perform near to human intelligence, there is still a lot of room for improvement. Machine learning models require loads of training datasets, and these should be of high quality as well. Data is not always available which makes the training process difficult and machine learning models start to make predictions that might not be suitable for human beings.

Machine learning requires a lot of resources and time to develop algorithms and complete the training process. As we can achieve a considerable amount of relevance and accuracy, there are several other functions and external resources required to avail maximum outcome from the machine learning models. Furthermore, interpretation of results might not be accurate in all cases, as humans are not completely aware of the functionality of machine learning models and how they are yielding predictions.

Machine Learning vs Data Science

Artificial intelligence and data science are major technologies in today's world. Although artificial intelligence is involved in data science operations, it definitely does not completely represent artificial intelligence. Data science involves various underlying data operations and supports both structured and unstructured data. In artificial intelligence, there is a limited implementation of machine learning algorithms and we are required to use vectors and embeddings.

Generally, data science is widely used in advertising, Internet search engines, and marketing industries whereas artificial intelligence models are more focused on manufacturing, healthcare, transportation, and robotics projects. Artificial intelligence and data science models can also be combined together for boosting the performance of machine learning systems. Data has become an essential factor for each industry and business for which companies are focused on developing secure storage systems as well.

Data science covers various fields such as programming, mathematics, and statistics. For data scientists to develop the best performing data science models though Python programming, getting information and accurate training datasets is immensely important. Moreover, other steps involved in data science including maintenance, visualization, manipulation, and extraction of data to forecast predictions, and occurrence of future events is also a major part of data science model development approach.

Most of the traditional artificial intelligence and machine learning algorithms were provided with goals in advance. With the evolution and development of the deep learning approach, data scientists have been able to understand the patterns and get valuable insights from data in a better way.

Differences and Constraints

There are considerable differences between artificial intelligence and machine learning. Computer systems still do not have consciousness and full autonomy like human beings which makes it difficult for data scientists to achieve one hundred percent accurate results from machine learning systems. Instead, the models only perform tasks for which they are trained, whether they are for the benefit of humans or not. Data science is the study and analysis of data, and a data scientist is responsible for outcomes the model will be delivering in the industry.

Moreover, the main requirement of data science models is to process data and complete other activities like transformation and cleaning. Artificial intelligence is a tool for data scientists and it is the best available approach to analyze data. On the other hand, data scientists are also held accountable for reviewing patterns in data by applying predictive modeling techniques. Depending on the requirements, the limitations and constraints of data science models can be managed to achieve accurate data insights and analytics in the future.

Different statistical techniques are used in data science models whereas in artificial intelligence, we take support from computer algorithms. Data science is all about finding hidden patterns in data, whereas artificial intelligence concepts are based on the autonomy and performance of machine learning models.

Useful Deep Learning Methods and Techniques

Learning about the advantages of transfer learning and latent features of pre-trained architecture can help you gain better insights and predictions from deep learning models. Remember that pre-trained weights are a good option to be considered as compared to the randomly initialized weights because they can be easily modified. Furthermore, we can also limit weight sizes and absolute value of weights to generalize the machine learning model. In this way, you can achieve maximum output and performance from your training data as well.

Moreover, you can also change the output layer and replace model defaults with a specific output size and activation function which is best suited for your domain. Make sure that you do not remove the first layers of a neural network because they are responsible for interpreting features and performing interactions throughout the domain as well.

Quality Assurance

Optimizing deep learning and machine learning models is quite simple if you are well aware of the design, algorithms, and functionality of the model. Hyperparameter settings and optimization algorithms make it easier to check the performance of a machine learning model and are ideal for conducting quality assurance checks as well. Each model is based on a specific set of hyperparameters which include number of hidden layers, number of neurons, activation functions, and optimization algorithm. Moreover, other factors such as learning rate, regularization hyperparameters, and regularization techniques are best for conducting in-depth quality checks for a machine learning model.

Most of the time, quality assurance mechanisms are not recognized by some artificial intelligence and machine learning systems. To avoid such problems, we are required to research and select the best approaches to test each machine learning model separately. Using training data to overview the performance and prediction capabilities of a machine learning model is absolutely not recommended because it might not yield accurate results in each case. Understanding statistical techniques for data such as mean, median, and mode will be helpful in reviewing data relationships at a high level.

As the machine learning model gets trained, it is likely to make accurate predictions and data insights for any scenario. Model testing is mandatory because machine learning systems are implemented in information systems of businesses and companies of each category. As they are subject to handle critical data, we have to make sure the information is never compromised or mishandled by the machine learning model. Although machine learning systems are not 100 percent accurate, we can surely improve the performance, safety, and reliability by regularly conducting quality checks.

Advanced AI

An artificial intelligence system can become super intelligent and perform activities for positive development in today's world. Powerful programming languages such as Python and R can be used to develop high end machine learning and artificial intelligence models which are capable of completing complex tasks without any hassle. Although advanced artificial intelligence can unleash the potential of machine learning systems, there are several consequences that need to be focused. As we all know, intelligent systems are given training through specific datasets and they might not make suitable predictions in each scenario, which in return can become harmful for humans.

Things to Remember

An efficient machine learning model has the capability to adapt unseen and new data. This approach can be done by generalizing the machine learning model development process for which you have to follow some specific rules and techniques. The model will better generalize if the data contains a wide spectrum of observations and is reliable by all means. To predict an accurate outcome, a machine learning model utilizes training data at first whereas the testing data is used afterwards.

Remember that machine learning, artificial intelligence, and deep learning will never take over a human level of intelligence and decision-making capabilities. In fact, the models are vulnerable to human mistakes and whenever an error is found in a machine learning system, the model is completely held accountable for the mistake. Most of the hard work for developing machine learning model lies upon data transformation.

Most of the effort and time is spent on feature engineering and data cleansing methods. These methods allow data scientists to uncover the hidden features in the training data sets so that a relationship can be developed between the layers, variables, and attributes within the machine learning model. Deep learning has achieved great acceptance in the real world because the models developed from deep learning can be implemented in a broad range of applications and fields.

Today, the use of machine learning and deep analytics has reached a new level of success and acceptance. Due to the consistent improvement and development in hardware systems, the performance, reliability, and security of machine learning models is also increasing which brings long term benefits to companies and businesses.

We should try to focus on the outcomes and predictions of machine learning models which are directly associated with human beings. Taking the example of a healthcare system, there is absolutely no room for errors or mistakes because the patient who is following instructions from the machine learning model is absolutely unaware about the negative effects in case the model delivers misleading information. Such is the case with the machine learning and artificial intelligence models that are implemented in autonomous vehicles or financial systems.

Although machine learning, deep learning, and artificial intelligence models are reliable, they might never meet the level of human intelligence because computer systems are absolutely unaware about external factors associated with humans such as ethics or relationships. If a model is programmed to perform a specific task, it will keep on learning and developing predictions to achieve best outcomes even if it is bringing loss for humans.

Machine learning algorithms provide intelligent services and products which have delivered great advantages to humans.

Data analytics and deep learning are key factors that can directly affect the prediction capabilities of a model. To implement these strategies into a business model, we need to understand the core requirements of the business and implement the techniques and machine learning algorithms that can help in achieving the highest return on investment. Deep learning algorithms can bring long term advantages to businesses and humans in real life as well. Through accurate predictions and data insights, machine learning models serve as a best source for automating processes and tasks that were previously done through traditional computer systems. To achieve desired results, data scientists always focus on the maintenance and training of machine learning systems.

Conclusion

Python Data Analytics: How to learn python data science and use python machine learning. Introduction to deep learning to master python for beginners is a comprehensive guide for learning Python for machine learning and artificial intelligence. The concepts and methodologies explained in this book can be adopted to understand how data science actually works and why Python is the best programming language to develop high performing machine learning and data analytics models. Designed for beginners, we have explained each aspect and portion of Python programming language with code samples which will greatly help our readers in developing machine learning models.

Machine learning has revolutionized business processes and the way we are performing routine activities. By learning the basics and findings of data science, researchers can understand the functionality of machine learning systems and implement their Python programming skills to develop high end data science models. *Python Data Analytics: How to learn python data science and use python machine learning. Introduction to deep learning to master python for beginners* is absolutely easy to understand as it is intended to help beginners in learning core concepts of Python machine learning, data analytics, and data science with the support of examples and real-life scenarios.

References

(2019). What is Data Analytics?. Retrieved from https://www.mastersindatascience.org/resources/what-is-data-analytics/

Assessing Data and Creating a dataset, (2017). Retrieved from https://wp.wwu.edu/machinelearning/2017/01/29/accessing-data-and-creating-a-dataset/

Chris, N. (2019) A Beginner's Guide to Neural Networks and Deep Learning. Retrieved from https://skymind.ai/wiki/neural-network

James, W. (2028). Big Data VS Traditional Data. Retrieved from http://customerthink.com/big-data-vs-traditional-data-what-to-know-when-it-comes-to-defines-big-data/

Jason, B. (2018). Your First Deep Learning Project in Python with Keras Step-By-Step. Retrieved from https://machinelearningmastery.com/tutorial-first-neural-network-python-keras/

Machine Learning Algorithms. Retrieved from https://www.datarobot.com/wiki/algorithm/

Moussa, T. (2018). Lessons Learned from Building Scalable Machine Learning Pipelines. Retrieved from https://techblog.appnexus.com/lessons-learned-from-building-scalable-machine-learning-pipelines-822acb3412ad

Victor, R. (2019). How To Develop a Machine Learning Model From Scratch. Retrieved from https://towardsdatascience.com/machine-learning-general-process-8f1b510bd8af

www.ingramcontent.com/pod-product-compliance
Lightning Source LLC
Chambersburg PA
CBHW071127050326
40690CB00008B/1372